Touchable

Touchable

SPIRITUAL INSIGHTS
FROM A TIME OF SUFFERING

BRIAN BARBER

ISBN Paperback: 978-0-578-20263-1

Printed in the United States of America. Also available as a Kindle edition.

Cover and Interior Design: Ghislain Viau

To Laura, my wife and partner in life. Our journey in this world continues. God has carried us through our darkest waters yet. Let us trust Him to carry us the rest of the way into His bright Kingdom.

Contents

About This Book

You won't find extraordinary writing in this book, writing that emerges out of a lengthy and arduous struggle to present my thoughts succinctly, with great precision. You won't find tight paragraphs or perfectly chosen words. What I hope you find are raw, unfiltered insights.

Over the previous two years or so, these insights seemed to come to me in whole form, and the struggle was to quickly transfer them to paper intact. When an insight revealed itself, I tried my best to stop, get quiet, deeply connect with the thoughts and feelings and then capture them on paper in that moment. I didn't want to wait and reflect back on the experience and then record my reflections. What mattered was the "now". The writing was an exercise at preserving what had just shown up more than it was an effort at shaping it.

So, the primary importance here is not so much the writing as it is the integrity of the insight. This is a faithful record of what I was thinking and feeling right then and there as the storm swirled around me. Whatever emerged, emerged.

My words come out a little sloppy at times. And I repeat myself a little. Certain ideas and sentiments pop up over and over again. That can be annoying, and I imagine many will speak to me as they read: "okay, okay, I get what you're saying. Enough already." I was tempted to cull out the repetition. But I resisted that urge, fearing that would somehow sterilize the whole thing, processing all the nutrients out of it, leaving the whole thing less raw. And that is what I want to communicate: the raw insights born out of a dark storm Laura and I have weathered.

What we've been through can be expressed with words, but certainly can't be captured by them. Indeed, no suffering can. It is broader, deeper than that. It is wild and can't be caged or confined. It is grimy. I want that reflected in this book.

I did revisit each insight and tweak some words in an effort to communicate clearly. But I tried to keep that to a bare minimum so as not to lose the gamy taste of it all. A few insights came to me very thin at first – a short phrase or paragraph would come to mind, for instance. I would write it down, thinking there was not much there at the time, only later to realize something was there, below the surface, and it needed to come out. So, I would return to it and see what it was. But the thrust and force of each insight was received in a moment and, for the great majority of insights, the full expression of them was written in one sitting.

The writing had a quick pace to it. It was as if I could feel in my gut something taking shape. I wanted to let it out quickly before I lost it or mangled the whole thing by putting too much thought to it.

I pray God the insights found here are helpful to all and especially to those of you in the middle of your own dark storm. Hopefully you come to see that what you are feeling and thinking is what others feel and think while the storm rages. And hopefully you begin to see, while under dark clouds, the wonderful hope – indeed, the sure reality of the wonderful hope we have in Christ. For in Him, nothing is for nothing – all suffering has a purpose – and all will be well. At His appointed time, He will call each one of us to Himself, to the Kingdom of God, and we will step into unending joy and peace in His presence. As the words of the great hymn speak so beautifully: "Be still my soul. Thy best, thy heavenly friend through thorny ways leads to a joyful end."

January 7, 2018

Back Story

A routine annual checkup in May, 2015, revealed my wife Laura was suffering from severe anemia. Unable to point to a likely cause of the low hemoglobin numbers, our physician immediately put us in touch with a hematologist to run more extensive blood work. Those labs turned up a high marker for cancer. In an instant, just like that, our life changed.

The hematologist told us he wanted Laura to have a bone marrow biopsy, the first of six she would get over the next 18 months. The first biopsy attempt – done without anesthesia – was excruciatingly painful. Her sister Marcia and I were in the room as the physician assistant struggled to extract marrow through a needle she inserted into Laura's hip. Laura screamed out as I have never heard before. And our PA was unable to extract any marrow. Marrow is gelatinous and normally extracts easily. That told us something was very wrong in her bones.

We scheduled a second biopsy, this time at a hospital to be performed under sedation. The doctor extracted a good marrow sample and we waited another week for the laboratory results.

By the time we got to the hematologist appointment to hear the biopsy results, it had been three weeks; three weeks knowing something was terribly wrong with Laura's bone marrow, but not knowing what exactly was going on. Our imaginations were spinning. Was it cancer? The chances were very high that it was. How serious was it? We didn't know. Was it treatable? We didn't know. Was I in real danger of losing her? That was a real possibility.

At our appointment, Dr. S confirmed our fears. The biopsy uncovered extreme fibrosis of the bone marrow, a common feature of aggressive cancers of the bone and blood. "Something is wrong, but I don't know what it is," remarked the doctor. "I need to have the lab run more tests before I can know what we are facing."

Our hearts sunk. We were in trouble and it would take another week before we would know what was going on. That week may have been the worst week of my life up to that point. It was difficult to work, to concentrate. The hours crawled along. I found myself crying throughout the day. I would gasp for air for no reason as a shudder of fear would sweep through my body. Darkness seemed to be swallowing me up.

"You have Myelofibrosis," the doctor reported at our next appointment. It is a disease of the bone marrow that is the result of a gene mutation. This mutated gene in the marrow begins to multiply. As it multiplies it takes over space that, in a healthy bone, is populated by healthy blood cells, the very cells tasked with creating red blood cells, white blood cells and platelets. These healthy cells slowly get crowded out, leaving the marrow no longer able to produce enough blood. As the disease progresses, the patient becomes dependent on blood transfusions to survive, as many as 3 a week in the advance stages. Eventually, unable to produce blood, the victim dies.

There is no cure for this disease.

It is technically not a cancer and therefore the risk of it metastasizing to the rest of the body is zero. However, it can, in rare cases, transform into a virulent form of leukemia.

"I want you to get a sonogram of the abdomen," instructed Dr. S. As the disease progresses, the spleen begins to enlarge. He wanted to know if Laura's spleen was being affected, a measure of how advanced the disease is. The sonogram revealed her spleen was normal, showing no signs of enlargement. The disease was not advanced.

Though there is no cure, there is still hope. The only path for survival leads to a bone marrow or stem cell transplant. Without a transplant, the patient dies. So, the hematologist arranged for us to meet with a transplant doctor as soon as possible.

"In my opinion you are going to be in serious trouble in two to four years", declared the transplant doctor. "We need to think about a transplant pretty soon." We were in shock. In a span of a little over 8 weeks we had gone from "you are anemic" to "you need a bone marrow transplant". A bone marrow transplant? This is one of the most difficult and risky procedures you can have. People die from them. In an instant we were placed on a path to transplant. It was real. Our destiny was set.

The disease was not advanced, but it was advancing. In a matter of two months, Laura started receiving blood transfusions. Her hemoglobin levels were routinely hovering around the danger level and a blood transfusion would temporarily boost them. But the effects were temporary. A month after transfusion, she would be back in the hospital receiving another one. This continued for nine months.

During those months the transplant team began their search for a donor for Laura. They tested Laura's siblings for a match. Transplants with sibling donors are the least risky and have the best track record of success. No luck. So, they turned to searching the hundreds of donor registers that exist all around the world for a match. They look at ten factors. The team seemed confident they would find a ten-out-of-ten match.

About eight weeks into the search, the team was getting a little concerned. Typically, with Caucasian patients, a match pops up within the first month. But no luck. Our patient coordinator told us Laura's genetic profile was a little unique; that she must have some out-of-the-ordinary ethnicity in her blood line. Our hearts sunk a little. Laura's great paternal grandmother was reportedly native American. This was throwing a wrench in the works. They do perform successful transplants with donors who are a nine-out-of-ten match. They are more risky and carry a higher likelihood the patient will suffer from graft versus host disease (GVH), a condition in which the new immune system (the graft) attacks the patient's body (the host).

A few more months ticked by as they sought a donor. We were in a holding-pattern routine of monthly transfusions. Only the transfusion rate was increasing. By now Laura was receiving one every three weeks. The disease was advancing.

During a regular appointment with our transplant doctor in San Antonio, Dr. Z, we got the word: "The dark clouds are gathering and we need to go to transplant now. We will have to go with the best match we can find." We shuddered because we knew what that meant. We would have to go to transplant with a nine-out-of-ten match. One of the most difficult and dangerous medical procedures on the planet and we were stepping into it with a strike against us.

We were not prepared for this. It is one thing to face this daunting challenge with a ten-match. We knew it would be hard and scary, but we had a sense that we would get through it, that it would be successful. But going to transplant with a nine-match – well, all bets are off in that case. Now I was truly afraid. I knew the odds had just gone up that her body would reject the donor stem cells and Laura would die. If she lived, the chances were higher she would have severe GVH and possibly for the remainder of her life. The storm clouds seemed to grow darker by the day.

On June 12, 2016, we gathered up our suitcases and took off for Methodist Hospital in San Antonio Texas to undergo a stem cell transplant. I remember Laura walking up to the garage apartment to say good-by to her sister, Marcia. She had been living up there since October of 2013. Marcia was diagnosed with stage-four lung cancer in April of that year. Being single, with no kids, living by herself in California, we knew she would need someone to help her get through the treatment regimen she was about to undergo. So, we moved her into the apartment so we could take care of her. She was in remission until a month earlier when the cancer had reappeared, this time in her brain. As Laura walked into the apartment, she looked at Marcia and said "We're going to make it. We're both going to make it through this, you and I." They hugged and Laura left.

That day is seared in my mind. On the drive to San Antonio we stopped by a McDonalds for a quick egg McMuffin and a coffee. There was something comforting, something normalizing about going through the drive through and getting some breakfast. On some level we were reaching for our old life, reaching for some assurance that everything was normal and okay.

As we parked and walked to the registration desk at the hospital, I felt like a convicted man presenting himself to prison officials to serve out his term. I knew the hospital was to be our home for the next month. Once admitted, Laura will not leave the floor of the hospital for about 30 days. In preparation for the actual transplant, she is given a week's worth of chemotherapy using the strongest drug they have. She receives two doses a day. This destroys her bone marrow and leaves her completely vulnerable to infection. Not only that, if she were to badly cut herself during this period, she would be unable to clot the wound because her body is no longer producing platelets that do the clotting. She would be at risk of bleeding to death.

Once underway, she must stay on the transplant floor, which is a sterile environment. It takes at least 21 days after transplant for the new stem cells to find their way into the bone marrow and set up shop to beginning manufacturing healthy blood again. Until that happens, she is trapped on the transplant floor of the hospital.

On Saturday, June 18, she received her transplant. A nurse comes to her room with a large syringe of the donor's stem cells (collected from the donor the day before and flown in that night). She connects the syringe to Laura's port in her chest and begins to slowly infuse them into her body. It takes a little over 20 minutes.

All goes well. Every day after the transplant they would draw blood and run labs. They were watching to see if her blood counts (hemoglobin, white blood cells, platelets) would recover. If they did, she would likely survive. If they didn't, she would not. Around day 5 the numbers started ticking up.

Then she encountered a problem. Ten days out she was experiencing unrelenting nausea. This was unexpected and not normal. It went on for 4 or 5 days and the doctors could not figure out why it was happening. Laura couldn't even drink a glass of water without throwing it back up. At one point during the nausea, she turned to me and said "Am I dying?". I was scared.

One of the doctors suggested Laura get a brain scan and that is when they discovered the problem. The back portion of Laura's brain was swollen. She was having a rare reaction to the immune suppressing medication she was on. They immediately withdrew the medication and within 24 hours the nausea abated.

Laura had very severe soars in her mouth, a very common occurrence in transplant patients. It was so severe that she could barely swallow. They had to hook her up to a suction tube to evacuate the saliva from her mouth. Every 5 minutes or so, Laura would have to put the wand in her mouth and close her mouth around it. This went on for a little over a week.

As the days passed, Laura's blood counts continued to rise. The transplant was taking. Laura's donor cells were in the bone and were manufacturing blood. To say we were relieved is an understatement. Some people go through this process and the new stem cells, for whatever reason, never take hold. The body rejects them. That places the patient in a very dangerous situation that is difficult to survive. But Laura was improving and the transplant was working.

Saturday, July 12 we left the hospital. The initial phase of the transplant was a success. Her body was producing blood. Laura was very weak, to the point where I had to hold onto her when she walked. Her legs were weakened from the high levels of steroids she was on and she had lost nearly 25 pounds. She needed to gain weight and start getting her strength back.

We were out of the hospital, but we could not go home to Austin. We had to move into an apartment in San Antonio 30 minutes away from the clinic. For the next 6 - 8 weeks we would have to visit the clinic so they could draw blood and run labs to monitor her blood. For the first week, we went every morning. She was doing well. After the first week, Dr. Z let us come 3 times a week for the next two weeks. She continued to improve, so much so that he authorized us to go home to Austin for the weekend. We spent three weeks living in the apartment in San Antonio during the week, visiting the clinic every other day, and heading home for the weekend. All seemed to be going well.

Then it all turned on us. Laura had a rough Sunday night where she was up about every 45 minutes with diarrhea. We called the doctor the next morning. He asked us to come in that day to the clinic. At our appointment, he told us he believed it was GVH disease, that Laura's new immune system was attacking her body. He increased her steroid dosage and we went back to the San Antonio apartment. It didn't seem to help. We called him the next day and told him. He increased her dosage again. Next day, same thing – no improvement. He increased her dosage yet again. No improvement. This went on all that week, each day the doctor increasing her steroids, but it had little effect. Eventually, on Sunday, he admitted her back into the hospital. He scheduled her for a colonoscopy and endoscopy on Monday morning. He wanted to know how severe the GVH was.

We got the results of the scopes Tuesday morning at 7:00 a.m. We were still sleeping when the PA came in to tell us. "You have grade-4 GVH in your lower intestine," she said. "If you respond to the treatment, you will be fine." What she didn't tell us was if she didn't respond to the treatment, she would die. Of those who contract grade-4 GVH after transplant, 80% die. We were in serious trouble. The treatment consists of massive doses of steroids over several weeks and even months. All we could do was pray and hold on. It was totally out of our hands at this point.

They began administering large doses of intravenous steroids. Within two days it appeared she was responding positively. Her condition was not worsening; in fact, it was subsiding ever so slightly. That was wonderful news. As the days passed she steadily improved. She was responding to the treatment.

But we weren't in the clear yet. Maybe 10 days into our second hospital stay – I think it was a Wednesday – I noticed Laura was struggling to perform very basic tasks. She could not remember how to work her cell phone to the point that I had to coach her how to make a call. She forgot how to work the remote control for the television. She noticed it as well. We wrote it off as an annoying effect of the many medications she was on.

The next day, however, she slipped into episodes of psychosis. Everything scared her. Even I scared her. She would look at me and say "you're scaring me" and ask me to get away. Then she would ask me, through tears, not to leave her, over and over again. I would assure her I wasn't going to leave her and it didn't help. She was inconsolable, terrified I was going to abandon her. An hour later she would tell me I was scaring her and would ask me to leave the room.

The nurses were watching all this and got the doctors involved. They immediately sent Laura down for her second brain scan. Their hunch was right: the base of her brain was swollen...again! She was having her second bought with PREZ, that rare reaction some patients have to immune suppressing medication. Her first episode, during the initial hospital stay after transplant, she experienced unrelenting nausea. This time she was experiencing psychotic episodes. The scan revealed the swelling was much more extensive than her previous episode. Once again they discontinued the medication immediately. They monitored her very closely and I could tell they were concerned. Her psychosis immediately stopped. It took another week for her brain to recover, but it did.

She would spend 5 weeks in the hospital recovering from the GVH. I never left her side, sleeping on a cot by her hospital bed at night. The day we left the hospital, she was very thin – 108 pounds. She went in for transplant weighing 138.

That was the same day we learned that her sister, Marcia, who was in California for cancer treatments, was going to be sent to hospice care. Her cancer was getting worse rapidly and there was nothing more the doctors could do for her. They gave her a few weeks to live.

Laura's heart was crushed beyond description. She would never see her sister again. I was crushed too. I had come to really get to know Marcia and love her over the last 3 years. She was part of our life. In fact, we had become a family: me and Laura and Marcia and her dog Rita. And now she was dying.

It was two weeks later, on September 29, we got the call from hospice that Marcia had passed away. The weight was so heavy that it was hard to see how Laura could bear up under it all. Her body, weak and battered from the transplant – and now her spirit crushed with the loss of her sister whom she loved so deeply.

Those were our darkest days. Laura was so physically depleted that she couldn't write. Her hands would shake so that she could not steady the pen. I would have to write for her. We were in San Antonio in a small two-bedroom apartment, holding on as best we could, separated from home and friends.

And that is when we began to read scripture at night. I suggested to her, one day, that we spend 15 minutes each night just reading some scripture. She wanted to do that. It became a lifeline for both of us, but especially for her. During those dark days, she would tell me that the only time she didn't feel afraid was when we were reading scripture at night. She would wait all day for that time together, listening to me read. It was the only thing that brought her peace. It was the only thing that calmed her fear.

Laura continued to improve and in a matter of a few weeks we were out of the apartment and back home in Austin. It was great to be home, but very hard without Marcia living in the apartment. And our struggles were not yet over.

The morning of Friday, December 23 Laura walked into the kitchen complaining that her leg really hurt. I thought little of it. Thirty minutes later I find her in bed, watching television. "Your leg still hurts?" I questioned. "Yes, and now it's tingling." That was not a good sign. I asked her to pull the covers away and let me look at it. What I saw scared me. Her leg was beginning to turn purple. I knew this was serious. We called our transplant doctor in San Antonio. "Get her to the emergency room. Sounds like she has a blood clot." I helped her out of bed and she went in to get dressed. But she was struggling. She was having a hard time standing up. I was helping her stand while at the same time working to get her pants on. "Let me sit down." She sat down and then just couldn't quite get up again. Now we were in trouble. I quickly realized we weren't going to get her to the car for a trip to the hospital, so I grabbed the phone and called 911. When the paramedics arrived, they took her blood pressure – 65 over 40 (I don't remember the exact reading, but it was in that range). She was in serious danger. They worked to stabilize her as best they could and loaded her into the ambulance. I followed…. scared!

At the hospital, they rushed her to the back and immediately drew blood for labs. A doctor came in and told us it appeared she had a blood clot, but they didn't know how severe it was. They ordered a sonogram of her leg.

To everyone's surprise, the sonogram came back negative – no sign of a clot or blockage. The doctors spent an hour trying to figure out what was wrong with her. It wasn't until they took another look at the sonogram that they discovered the problem. She indeed did have a blood clot in her leg – a clot that extended up the entire length of her leg! It was so large, they missed it on the sonogram.

She underwent surgery a few hours later and spent the next forty-eight hours in intensive care as they closely monitored her condition. We spent Christmas eve and Christmas day in intensive care. Monday morning, the doctors confirmed the clot had broken up and Laura was going to be fine. She was released that afternoon.

Her recovery is a little bumpy and slow, but she is moving in the right direction and making consistent progress. She receives treatments every month for GVH and that will likely continue for another 6 months or more. She is back to a good weight and her hair has grown back – curly and dark. Her blood factor numbers are all in normal ranges. She is working, eating well, and going about her normal daily routine. She has a painful hole in her heart from losing Marcia that will never fully heal. And we are not sure what the future holds with regard to her recovery from the transplant. But we continue to read scripture every night and are learning – for the first time in our life together – to release things, as best we can, to God and fully trust Him, as best we can, for the future.

October, 2017

1

Blind by Blessing

Before Laura's diagnosis, life was a fierce blessing, and I did not recognize it as such. Going through the day was effortless. It was all so safe and wonderful that much of my day was played out on an unconscious, automatic level. I moved through my world much like an airliner on auto pilot. I was beset by annoyances, true, but it turns out that is all they were – just minor annoyances. I was light on my feet. I breathed the air with ease. My mind would drift off into day dreams and future imaginings. And when I would bump up against some unwelcome turn of events, I would stumble around a bit, but I wouldn't fall.

Life here in this country is so easy and comfortable for many of us. We are insulated from harsh elements – from heat or cold; from rain and wind; from the pounding sun. I spend much of my day on solid surface and dry ground. When I'm hungry, I open the refrigerator; when I'm thirsty I turn on the kitchen faucet. When I'm dirty, I take a warm shower. And when I'm tired, I fall onto a comfortable, plush bed and lay my head on a fat pillow. I'm asleep in a matter of minutes.

But something dank and difficult lurks beneath all this comfort. And when we received Laura's diagnosis, it emerged with a blinding darkness and I saw for the first time the reality of all this. This is not heaven or God's Kingdom. This is indeed what the Apostle Paul labels "the domain of darkness". And we had fallen into it head long.

Blessing and comfort blinded me. I was living a life of deception. The conditions of my life, before the disease, were good. All was pleasant and in place. It led me to the false belief that life is, at its heart, in its bones, pleasant and in place.

Disrupt the blessing, however, and eyes are opened, and mine were, really for the first time in my life. Laura's disease brought immediate clarity. Nothing is sure. Everything I thought was solid turns out to be unstable. I never gave a moment's thought to disease. And yet here it was, crashing into our world.

The effect was that it undercut everything I trusted as solid. That is the nature of affliction. It spills out into every facet of life. We had been touched by life-threatening disease. One would expect that to shatter a belief that disease would never touch us, while leaving us feeling safe in all other domains of life. No, it didn't work that way. I instantly knew that if disease can touch us, absolutely anything can touch us. That means we are vulnerable to natural disaster, accident and personal tragedy, crime and violence, and financial ruin. It turns out the dangers of this earthly existence cannot be conveniently compartmentalized and cordoned off. If one unthinkable hardship touches me, then all unthinkable hardships can touch me. My safe world has collapsed and now no place is safe. Now, no matter where I am or the favorable conditions I enjoy, any affliction can, at any point in time, reach out and take away my comfortable life. There is no place to hide.

On the other side of disease, I see this all so clearly. The scales drop from my eyes and the world comes into sharp focus. The true, harsh nature of this life is revealed. Yet why did I not see this before? I know the teaching of the scriptures. This world is the domain of darkness, the valley of the shadow of death. This existence is fraught with all kinds of peril. We are all vulnerable to this fallen world. Why was I blind to this?

Honestly, I can't imagine how I could possibly come to this understanding independent of being touched by this affliction. This is a knowledge that is not acquired through thought, but rather through experience. It took the destructive force of disease to demolish my safe place. It took the blinding light of disease to bring true sight. This is, in part, why God allows suffering, for it alone has the power to bring us to the truth about this life. That is, for all the creature comforts we enjoy, for all the predictability that characterizes our daily routine, for all the protections out there in this country that serve as shields behind which we hide, we are naked out in the world. And there is nothing – absolutely nothing – we can do to make us invulnerable from even the worst imaginable. We are weak and exposed and there simply is nothing we can do about it.

Well, that may be an overstatement. There is one thing we can do, but only one thing. We can flee to God. We can take hold of the glorious truth that He is sovereign over all this world and that this life – this grimy, scary trek – is not all there is. I am an eternal soul. My final destiny is not death on this earth but eternal life in the Kingdom of God. This life is a prelude, a preview of coming attractions. My true home is with God in His eternal kingdom.

Now, if that is true, it changes the equation. It is still the case that I may well experience affliction and great suffering in this life. But now, knowing God not only reigns over my world but has destined me for eternal life in His presence in His eternal kingdom someday, suffering takes on a new feel. No longer a tragic random accident, I now can endure it as coming upon me from within the sovereign oversight of God. I can hold onto the real hope that God allows it for a great purpose, an eternal purpose. And should my suffering swallow up my life, I need not despair, for this life is temporary and not all there is. Suffering does not ever have the final say. God has the final say. God will raise me to eternal life someday. Then all suffering and hardship will be complete and I will step into my highest life and true destiny: the eternal Kingdom of God.

On that day my eyes will be opened again, and for the final time. I will see the glory and wonder of this creation and the true beauty of life that my fleshy eyes simply cannot see. I will see all things clearly as everything will stand in sharp focus before me. On that day I will finally be truly shielded from disease, and hardship, and tears, immune from it all. I will never again fear what may come my way. Finally, on that day, all tears have dried, all hardship is over and disease and tragedy and violence and disaster are no more. My long journey on earth is complete…..God and life have won!

June 7, 2016

2

Surrender To Hope

I t is a strange thing to admit – and even stranger to hear myself admit it – but I have resisted hope all my life. Without realizing it, I have shied away from taking hold fully of the great aggregate hope that is mine in Christ: the wonderful hope of eternal life after death; of resurrection into an imperishable body that will never decay or fade. I gave intellectual assent to it all, much like signing off on a creed. I accepted the assertions that I will see Him face to face and live with Him for all eternity; that I will one day live here on earth in the Kingdom of God with Christ ruling supreme and, on that day, take possession of all creation as an heir of God; that I will be reunited with loved ones again someday in Christ; that there will come a day when all tears and pain and suffering and hate and evil and violence will be no more and peace and joy will reign uninterrupted forever.

I accepted these truths. But – and this is the real crux of the matter – I discovered that I didn't really believe them deep in my soul, deep in my heart and mind. They weren't real like this chair I am sitting on is real. They weren't real like my beating heart. They weren't real like playing the piano is real. It turns out all along this hope was only "kind of real", only "somewhat real", only "mostly real". And it was Laura's disease crashing in on me that drove all of that truth to the surface.

It took me by surprise, frankly. If someone were to question me about all this, I would without hesitation say "yes, I believe all that". But something was missing. Now I understand. I have resisted really, deeply believing all this wonderful hope because it is, frankly, crazy talk. It is toddler talk. It is the stuff of fairy tales and nursery rhymes. No adult can really take that kind of talk seriously. Can they?

When I look out into this world I see a lot of grime and dirt. I experience a hard reality that has no room for such silliness. The hope is so fantastic, it is near impossible to believe it. Which makes it risky. For if I begin to give into it and lean hard on it, the ground might very well give way leaving me despondent, without hope. That state will be worse than the first. Better to not have hoped than to have hoped and been sorely disappointed.

After all, it could be that I have it all wrong and fundamentally misunderstand the scriptures around this topic. It could be I take all those wonderful hope passages in scripture too literally. All this stuff about the lion lying down with the lamb and a day when all tears will cease, and death will be no more. The sophisticated student of scripture would not be so gullible as to take all that literally.

The hope in Christ feels a lot like fantasy, the kind of fantasy I relished as a child. In fact, it strikes me that the world Christ will one day bring to this earth is, in many ways, the kind of world I lived in as a child. I was insulated from ugliness and evil and pain. All my needs were met abundantly and without me tending to them whatsoever. The world was safe and I filled my time taking in the wonder of it all, exploring and discovering new things. The adult world and all that mess out there was of no concern to me, as if it didn't even exist. That was truly a magical time.

The wonderful hope that I see in scripture is just like that. It is magical. It is unbelievable. It is fantastic beyond fantastic. These are promises that are incomparable. No world-view can begin to rival Christianity in all this. The scriptures hold out for me a destiny that is quite literally unbelievable. How can it possibly be true?

There is a part of me that longs to believe all of that is true. I feel my heart reach for a world and life that is as wonderful as I just described. This trial that Laura and I are going through has brought me to the end of me. I am broken, really for the first time in life. Hope in this life has been found to be empty. It has been snatched away from me. I am pulled into a mire of hard realities of disease and uncertainty and disappointment and fear and looming death and there simply is no space left for magic and childish wishing.

But all has changed in my life and now I cannot live, really live, without that magical hope. I didn't know that about me, but it is true. I look around at other people going through tragedy and pain and loss and they seem to be able to pull themselves together and face up to the challenge and face it all with courage and dignity. They manage to reconcile themselves to the harsh reality that life is hard and painful and everything we hold precious and dear is eventually taken away from us. Everything. It is taken away in this life through suffering. It is finally and forever taken away from us through death — of me or of those I love. Others seem to accept all this and get on with their life.

So what is wrong with me? Why can't I do that? I thought I was a strong person. When my day to suffer was upon me I thought I too would rise up with courage and press on in life. I would be someone others would admire and look at and say "now he is a strong man. That is how a person should face loss. Take it and get on with life". But that hasn't happened and I have failed. I am not strong in it. I am weak and emptied. I am not rising up to meet the challenge. I am collapsing. I am on the ground, on my knees. And I fear – how I hope this isn't true – I may never get to my feet again.

I am between a rock and hard place: afraid to hope for these "fantasies" of the faith, and yet unable to resign myself to giving up the hope that this life is not all there is and that something more, something so much greater, is still ahead for me….still ahead for Laura.

At some point in this struggle, the weight of it became too much and I broke: I gave in to hope. And that's when things began to change. Or maybe I should say, more accurately, that is when I began to change. It was clearly a supernatural work of grace. Somehow, at some point, I realized it was my pride keeping me from the hope. It is clear to me now that, even as a committed believer, I couldn't bear the thought of being one of those weaklings who "flee to heaven" when hard times come upon them because they haven't the inner strength to resist the childish longings for unending joy and peace in eternal life with God. Life on Earth becomes too hard so they turn all their attention to heaven and find consolation. That is a coward's way out. I am stronger than that. I won't succumb to my pain by fleeing to childish hope. Only weak people do that, people who need a placebo in life to help them cope with hard realities.

I was in a very strange and uncomfortable space. Here I was, claiming, and genuinely possessing, faith in Christ, while rejecting the great hope He offers.

So I broke. I raised the white flag in an act of surrender — a surrender to hope. I finally embraced all that foolish hope that is held out to us in Christ. Am I weak? Am I foolish? I don't believe so. In any case, the point is I reached a point where I could not go on and had to reach for the hope. Because, you see, I need that hope. This affliction showed me that I am one of those people that cannot cope with life without that hope. Not fantasy and not wishful thinking, but good, strong, real, adult hope that is in Christ. Life is simply unbearable for me without it.

And I am not alone, thank God, for the great body of hope that is contained in Christ is the safe haven to which storm-tossed Christians have fled for thousands and thousands of years. The New Testament authors time and time again bring the hope of eternal life and never-ending fellowship with God through Christ to those who are suffering. Those great truths strengthen us in hard times. They are meant to do so.

Indeed, I found the great hope we have in Christ to be the one thing — the only thing — that finally lifted me off the floor and stood me on my feet again. For all that we are suffering, there is coming a day when we will step into glory in the presence of God and all suffering will become a memory. And the glory and joy of that day will erase the memory of this pain and suffering much like the sun outshines a candle. With so great a hope, I can stand and walk, even in the midst of hardship and crushing loss, and finish this earthly journey into which God has sent me. For I know that my final destiny is eternal life, eternal peace, eternal joy with Christ in the Kingdom of God.

June 10, 2016

3

Always About My Soul

This affliction brings me back to the most basic truths of God for strength and solidity. It's as if I have to retreat to that faith space that is sure and unshaken: God lives and Christ died for me and rose again. He has me.

And even more basic is the truth that I am an eternal soul created by an eternal, personal, infinite God. For the moment I am interfacing with a physical creation from within a weak, decaying body. This experience is temporary and some day will be complete. When that day comes and God calls me to my eternal home, I will shed this mortal body and put on an immortal one. I, an eternal soul, will leave this present earth behind and cross over into everlasting life, finally at home in the Kingdom with my Father. The great truth – a most glorious truth – is my highest life is yet to come and the true "me" is yet to be revealed. They are realized on the other side of this life. For this life on earth is a journey of finite to infinite, of perishable to imperishable.

Because I am an eternal being, everything God does in my life has one aim in mind: the well-being of my soul, the core "me". This life is the servant of the eternal life that will someday be mine forever. It does not stand on its own and loses all meaning when disconnected from its eternal root. God is not so much concerned about the conditions of my life here and now as He is obsessed, if you will, with the health of my eternal soul.

Every trial is designed to secure some eternal good, namely, to grow my soul so that I might commune with God more wholly while on earth and be suitable, some inevitable day, for life before His unveiled presence in His eternal Kingdom. My current mortal life is a servant of eternal soul and that future eternal life and, as a servant, is expendable, if you will. Its mission is to bring about God's glory on earth and serve as a temporary home for eternal soul. But I, the core eternal "me", am not expendable. I am precious. My soul is precious. Suffering works to the benefit of my soul because it nurtures it and ultimately, somehow, enhances and enlarges my experience of eternity. God is more than willing to burden my life on earth for, in return, development of my soul. That is what I mean by "expendable": in His infinite wisdom He disrupts and even burdens my short-lived experience of life in order to grow my soul and heighten my eternal life experience, both on earth and, someday, in heaven. That is what gives meaning to suffering and pain: in the hands of God, I lose that which is temporal to gain that which is eternal.

June 16, 2016

4

The Deception of Appearances

Faith recognizes right off that all I see is not all there is. If I see, for instance, disease in my life – Laura's myelofibrosis – it appears to be destructive, evil. And, of course, on the level of divine creation and perfect will, it is evil. God never intended disease to exist in His perfect creation. It found an entry point into creation through Adam's sin. God allows it and uses it for His glory, but it remains deeply offensive to Divine sentiment.

Now, however, as we walk through this fallen world in faith, disease serves the purposes of God – always! It only appears to be an outlier. In reality it is a divine vehicle used by God to achieve his unfathomable purposes. Everything God does and allows is like an arrow drawn on a bow in His hands, pointing to some eternal good He wills to bring about.

But my sight deceives me. I see only hardship and suffering and destruction and tragedy. That is the deception of appearances according to 18th century saint Jean-Pierre de Caussade. Disease, as with other evils, is a disguise, a true deception. It appears composed of only evil. But it masks divine purposes, being an agent of eternal achievements and, ultimately, glory. In the end, I will look back at disease and all evil, as will we all, and see the incomprehensible wisdom and love of God. I will see how He makes a mockery of it, using it to advance His holy, glorious aims, and such aims as redound to my glory and good throughout all eternity – the deeper the valley, the higher the mountain. God will turn evil and tragedy on their heads, transforming them into agents of highest joy and glory for those who suffer under them in this life.

And just how is it possible for a man to see behind these deceptions to the great reality of divine providence that moves through them? That answer, at least, is clear. It is by the eyes of living faith that a man sees. The trick here is that it, more times than not, takes suffering to bring life to those eyes, to sharpen them that they may indeed see God behind it all. I have to look into mystery and the invisible, into the very throne room of the Lord. And to do that, the flesh has to be pushed aside. It is very near impossible to push it aside while I am kicked back in an easy chair, covered in comfort. It takes pain and loss and heartache to force me out of the chair in search of something solid and enduring. Once I step out, in desperation, in search of that, having been pushed by the suffering I have encountered, I am on the path of seeing. My eyes are undergoing the process of opening to faith.

This process of obtaining eyes of faith actually begins with faith and ends with faith. But thankfully I need only the smallest mustard seed of faith to begin the process. When the hardship falls on me, I have to muster some measure of faith, however feeble and small, to reach a trembling hand up toward heaven. God, in His infinite mercy, responds with grace at the most meager gesture. He rushes in and begins to nurture that faith seedling to grow and expand. And as He does that, my eyes begin to see, ever so faintly, the divine image of my God standing next to me in my grief and fear. At first I can barely make Him out. But as I stubbornly continue to reach for Him through tears, I see more clearly. He comes progressively more into focus and my heart and mind feel a peace that surpasses understanding overshadow them. My eyes of flesh are giving way to eyes of faith. And the deception of appearances is revealed. I come to understand that He holds all things in His hands, He redeems all sufferings and affliction......and all is well with my soul.

June 22, 2016

5

Losing Life to Save it

Through this affliction I am realizing that my stance toward life is captured by the notion I am here to live my version of my life. This is my life and I am the only one who can live it. That sums up what this is all about: I am to live my life fully my way.

Of course there is a grain of truth here. Yes, God would have me take hold and live my life. He gifted it to me and it is the only one of its kind. I am totally unique, a totally unique creation from the hand of The Most High. In all of human history, through the eons of time, I am the only "me" there will ever be. As such, I do have an obligation to God to live my unique life before Him and not conform or cow tow to social pressures. To acquiesce to the whims others entertain for my life is an affront to God: an affront to how He made me, when He made me, and where He placed me.

But the truth here is only a small grain. The rest is deception. I live because God has brought me into existence and continually sustains me. Were God to cease exercising this sustaining power, I would cease to exist. My very life, therefore, is first God's, not mine.

And add to that notion the fact that God has redeemed my life through the death of His Son, which means, once again, my life is no longer my own. Christ has paid my ransom and my life is His.

I am, therefore, to live God's version of my life. He alone has final say. He has twice over "earned" the right to play out His version of my life, whatever that may be. I am to glorify Him, and I do that by abandoning myself to His divine providence and wisdom, receiving humbly and thankfully what He decrees for me. If He wills I glorify Him with long life and comfort and great ease, He is to be praised and adored. And if He wills I glorify Him with a short life of struggle and affliction, He is to be no less praised and adored. In either case, I glorify Him, and that is the only measure of success for a life. To glorify Him is all that matters. The manner in which I achieve that is determined by God.

For me, losing my life has been an indispensable element of walking through this hardship. It has been really an abandoning of myself into the hands of God, surrendering to His grand purposes that are so over-arching as to be beyond my understanding. It is letting go, again and again, of this need I have – we all have – to "know and control" my life: I want to be able to control what I experience now and what I will experience in the future.

Of course, that I control my life is an illusion. Not a one of us exercises control over life like we imagine we do. For at any moment, at the blink of an eye, my life can change. I am one moment away from a totally different life than I imagined yesterday I would live. A diagnosis, an accident, natural disaster, violence, financial loss –all these can suddenly intervene to dramatically transform my life into something I could not have imagined and do not want. These unforeseen things have the power to take away my life forever and leave me with an unknown and seemingly unsafe future. And it is only by turning from this need to know and control my life and leaning into God's iron providence that I can adjust to what is in front of me – unanticipated and unwelcome as it is – to move forward with my new life.

If I hold onto my life at all cost, when one of these events crashes into me, I fall into despondency and resentment and bitterness. I likely collapse and fall out of life, withdrawing from it in a futile effort to push back against the irresistible force. This ruins me over time. And the irony is I push back in a desperate effort to save my life. I tell myself "this isn't happening" or "I will escape this soon" and console myself that my old life is not over at all, that this is simply a temporary interruption and I will get back to the life I must live. But my life as I have known and imagined it is indeed over – gone. And I must let it go by taking hold of God and, leaning on Him, embracing the new life in which I find myself. This is the act of losing my life and letting God save it by taking me forward into the new one in which He, in His divine wisdom, has sovereignly placed me. Like it or not, He has intervened and put to death my old life.

But God is infinitely and eternally faithful and loving. He never only takes away. He takes away in order that He might give back something all the more wonderful, more profound, more "in Him" than I would ever be able to attain any other way. Jesus teaches whoever wishes to save his life will lose it and whoever loses his life, for the sake of Christ (that is, to gain Christ), will save it. The purpose of losing life is that we might gain life. When He takes away, it is always in preparation for what He wants to give. And the new gift is more wonderful and beautiful than we could hope. Suffering is a one-way street forward, never backward. It is never the case that He brings suffering into my life to defeat or crush me or diminish my life. He brings it always with the aim that I might have life and have it more abundantly. Always!

In pursuit of losing my life to God, I have to also lose my perception of the nature of this life. This life on earth is not an end in itself. It is prelude, the great aim of which is the kingdom and eternal life with Christ before the Father. That is what I was created for. I was created to enjoy the greatest greatness that exists in the universe, namely, Christ Himself. I was not created for this world. God never intended I live in this flawed world trapped in this fragile, humble body. This current state of creation is fatally flawed and will one day pass away. Which means the life I live down here is neither my highest life nor my loftiest hope. It is not an end of itself; rather, it is a passing through, a temporary journey to a greater, enduring, eternal home. I am walking toward eternal life with God. My home is the Kingdom of God. That is my highest life and my sure destiny.

Therefore, I am not to raise this life up on a pedestal and worship it. I am not to approach it as a final destination; I am to approach it as a temporary journey. I am not to rest in it as my final home; I am to live in exile, treating this life as a temporary tent, reaching for my true home in the presence of God and Christ, longing to take my rest in God's kingdom. This life is not a resting place. It is a place of toil and effort and fatigue and struggle. It is a temporary and fleeting existence, a brief experience to lead me to eternity. I was made for the eternal Kingdom of God, not this temporal world of earth.

How does this impact my experience of suffering? Once I embrace life as a journey that ends at the throne room of God where I will forever enjoy fellowship with Him, I take a stand on eternal ground. Feet planted on solid rock, I am unmoved when temporal ground gives way. It will not take me down with it because my rock holds. My destiny is sure. My home is unshakable. The world around me crumbles, but I stand solid and strong because my soul, the very eternal, enduring essence of "me", is safe in God, invulnerable to the vicissitudes of life. Thus positioned, I can endure hardship knowing it is temporary and will not win out; knowing that life and love and joy win out. I am destined for eternal peace and rest and gladness in the presence of Christ and His Father. No amount of suffering can change that.

June 26, 2016

6

Not Meant For Dust

We live in a corrupt, decaying, diseased, evil world. To think we will get through it unscathed is foolish. All will be touched directly by the terrible effects of the fall of mankind – through natural disaster, disease, violence, injustice, personal tragedy; and through the life-long decay of our bodies, ending ultimately in death. None will escape.

Third-world cultures get this. Every day they confront the devastating effects of man's rebellion against God. When they wake up, they're hungry; when they go to bed, they're hungry. They live in unsanitary conditions which leave them quite vulnerable to all manner of disease. They fall victim to violence through crime and war. Life is grim.

But we who live in the modern industrialized world are insulated, in large measure, from the consequences of the fall. The state of the natural world out there is little more than a nuisance to us.

Rarely is it a life-threatening reality to be navigated every day. Our easy life conditions lull many of us into a belief that all is well with the world.

But all is not well. The world is deadly and unsafe, a state which God finds offensive. God originally created all things good, but that original creation was marred by man's rebellion against Him and we suffer for it to this day. By contrast, modern man understands this world as being neither out of phase nor corrupt. It is the way it is and it is natural, having always been this way. And, to the modern mind, this world will always be this way.

That explains their view or death. It is merely "what happens to be the case", what is. It is the natural and unavoidable dark partner of life – one simply cannot have one without the other. To him man is nothing more than a physical organism and death ends our life finally and forever.

To the Christian death is not on equal footing with life, as if it were simply the "other" actor on stage in this drama. Rather, it is an invader, unwelcome in God's perfect design, an offense to Him. To the modern, death is "baked into" this world, a natural result of evolution. To the Christian, death is completely unnatural, a foreign obstacle. To the modern, life and death are inextricably and forever welded together. To the Christian, death has no original claim on life. It is tolerated by God for the moment, but one day will be thrown off, cast out of this creation forever.

Given that death is as natural as life, modern man calls us to "be brave" in the face of it and face it with "courage". In "courage" we learn to accept what is and not let death leave us cowering in the corner. Those who face death courageously are lauded and lifted up as examples to follow.

The tragedy in this orientation lies in the fact that, courageous or not, death still comes. And once death takes me, I am gone forever, never to be again.

This courageous approach often includes strenuously ignoring death. We must keep it from our field of experience; ignore it for as long as possible. Yes, it will come, but not for a very long time, so why let it spoil the party? These misguided souls rush from distraction to distraction convincing themselves that somehow death is not real, that it plays no real role in their life. Others die, others suffer. We go to parties and enjoy life.

Other moderns, in the name of "courage", confront death head on. They well up with pride as they shake their fist at it and strike out robustly after life, fully aware that death might come at any moment and put an end to it all. Life is a treasure to be valued above all else and therefore held onto at all costs: it is, after all, all we have. These are the actors in the culture most admired and their well-respected stance in the face of death is nearly universally applauded.

Yet why exactly is that so admirable? How could courage be a nobler stance toward death than terror? In either case, once death comes, it finishes everything completely and forever. If this is true, how we face it is ultimately of no consequence one way or the other. One hundred years after my death, who will be around to tell the story of how courageous I was when my time came? And if my courage is remembered, how is that any more meaningful than if my terror is remembered? In either case I am no more forever. For the modern man, how he faces death is, in the end, as meaningless as how he lives life.

For me, I have more respect for the modern person who really sees the finality of it all and, because of their honest vision, admits to unspeakable fear and trembling at death. I think that is really the only sane response. "Courage" is irrational and meaningless if death is the end of it all.

Death is not the end of it all. In fact, we were never created to die. Man was created everlasting. We were not meant for dust. Death is an unwelcome intruder into God's creation. Our mortality is an aberration, an offense to God. We are eternal souls created by the eternal God. We never drop out of existence, for the life in us is the life of the Creator. He lives, therefore we live. If He were to cease to exist, we would perish.

Death does not have the final say. Indeed, death is, for the Christian, a home coming. It is the threshold over which we cross to enter our eternal home with Christ in the presence of the Father. Even Jesus refers to death as "departure", "going away", "sleeping". It is not a cessation of existence. It is a transition point that transports us out of this temporal world into the eternal world of God and Christ and the angelic realm. It is a door that opens for us. It is a pathway into the very presence of the eternal God. In Christ, we believers will know death as a glorious chariot that carries us home to be with our Savior and His Great Father.

June 27, 2016

7

Life to Glorify God

Through suffering I now see, with great clarity and hard conviction, that my life on earth has one simple purpose – to glorify God. And it is God who chooses exactly how my life will glorify Him. He orchestrates all events and circumstances and conditions toward that end. If He determines I am to glorify Him through a life of hardship and suffering, so be it. That is as meaningful and significant a life as one of great physical blessing and comfort. In fact, I now believe that a life of suffering may very well glorify God more than a life of comfort.

And God gives a special glory and grace to us who suffer. In His grace He brings it about that my experience of eternal glory in the Kingdom, when it is all said and done, will be all the more incredible because of the suffering I endure on earth. And that "benefit" from suffering will never diminish through eternity. Quite the contrary: it will be so fulfilling for me, the suffering I had to endure in this life will be as nothing in comparison. This is what the Apostle Paul is getting at when he exclaims "the sufferings of this present time are unworthy to be compared with the glory that is to be revealed to us."

The world evaluates this life by different measures. For the most part it scores life on the scales of achievement and success and self-actualization; the glory of God is of no significance. The more one achieves, the more successful one is, the more meaningful the life. The more one actualizes one's potential, the more successful one is. And the bigger the better. To achieve on a grand scale or to fully actualize oneself is to stand out as a most significant and meaningful life.

But achievement and self-actualization are of little to no worth from an eternal standpoint. The man who achieves great things in the business world, for instance, yet never comes to know God through Jesus Christ leaves a failed life behind. The woman who maxes out her personal potential yet never hears the voice of Christ leaves a failed life behind. To miss Christ and His Father is to miss the very purpose of life, which is to know and glorify God.

The world also lifts up longevity as a measure for a life. And that also is of no consequence to God. He is able to glorify himself as much by a brief life as by a long one. Christ proved that. His life was short by modern standards and yet the greatest, most significant life the world has ever known.

The world looks to good works as a measure of a life. The humanitarian is applauded. But good works, if not done unto God's glory, can be as self-glorifying as any other human pursuit, degrading into misguided acts of self-righteousness. Glorifying God is a matter of the heart more than activity. I can play a song on the piano and, with an attitude in my heart of offering the song up to God, play it to glorify Him. But if I play that same song with an attitude of "dig me", it fails to glorify Him. So too with good works. My heart must be humble before, and reaching up toward, God.

To glorify God is only right, for I owe Him everything. He created me; He spoke me into existence. He sustains me in life, moment by moment. He breaths my lungs and pumps my heart. When my basic needs in life are met, it is God who has met them for me. All that I have and all that I am – all is from God and in God. He has every right to spend my life as He will, for He rightly works all things after the counsel of His great will. If I live long or die young – God be glorified. If I enjoy pleasure or suffer pain – God be glorified. If I succeed greatly or fail miserably in life – God be glorified. When I come upon bad days of disease or violence or tragedy or disaster – whatever may come, the light of my life eternal is not diminished in the slightest degree and I can rightly glorify God. I now take great comfort in that fact.

God is the highest treasure of all and to glorify Him is the highest purpose for a life. If I live toward that end, I have done well. And when He decides my days are complete, He is the great Savior of my soul who calls me home to live with Him forever. That is a great glory to God.

June 28, 2016

8

Separate from Ordinary Life

The moment suffering crashes into me, through Laura's disease, I find I am instantly transferred into a life that is separate from ordinary life. All others that I see as I go through my daily, usual routine, continue to work their life as normal. They seem carefree and lighthearted. Their life is as safe and secure today as it was yesterday and they have no reason to believe it will be otherwise tomorrow. So, they put together vacation plans, run errands and enjoy daily pleasures – movies, dining out, shopping. All is well.

But I am now emotionally cut off from this kind of life and these activities and must deal with this disease – with hospitals and doctor visits and physical debilitation. The rest of the world continues to work a comfortable routine. But my routine has been upended. I am stripped of "lighthearted" and must carry a burden throughout the day, for months or even years – or possibly for the rest of my life. I am in a time of suffering, cut off from ordinary life and from others around me. My normal life is gone and I doubt I will ever see it again. I am alone in this, all alone.

This initial shock is powerful, almost terrifying. I feel I am drowning, gasping for air. I desperately try to keep my head above the waves. I wonder whether I will make it. The waters are heaving, churning, pounding me relentlessly. I am being pulled under and am powerless to escape.

At some point – I would say it was about 6 weeks into it – I begin to crawl out of the initial despair and find some solid ground. For 6 weeks I have been deepening into God. Every day, after dinner, up in the guest bedroom, I literally fall on the floor, face bowed down, and pray to God for mercy and grace. Slowly He lifts me and brings me to the truth that He is in this somehow; He is with us and He is faithful and trustworthy. Nothing is out of control; He remains in complete control of all circumstances in our life, even this one.

Slowly I open to the hope that there is purpose in this and – even more importantly for me – there is some benefit to this hardship, even if I can't see it yet. I am learning that there are some truths I simply cannot see from inside a normal life. These truths are illumined through suffering. And these truths are eternal, having to do with my relationship with Christ and the formation of my eternal soul, which explains, in part, why God is so willing to allow me to travel through the valley of the shadow of death. Everything He does aims at the health of my eternal soul. My life on earth is a servant, if you will, of my soul. That's the truth God brings to me. He uses my life on earth as an instrument of growth and deepening of my soul. My soul is His focus; my soul is most important to Him. It is the eternal treasure – the eternal "me" – for which He died.

As I walk further into this "not ordinary" life, I realize I have come to a fork in the road. I can resist this state of affairs in which I find myself. I can retreat into bitterness and resentment and spit at all of this. I can shake my fist and yell *"this is not fair and I won't stand for it. I want my old life back and I will not accept this new one."* I can fight against this reality…Or, I can surrender to it and accept, in faith, before God, that my previous life is gone and, like it or not, a new life is here. And this new life, for now at least, includes disease and pain and suffering. As frightening as it is, I have to let that old life die away. I have to turn, in faith, into this new one. I have no choice. I cannot go back.

And I have to face the fact that, not only is my old life dead, but I am dead as well. The carefree, relaxed, safe, lighthearted "me" is dead. I am now a "burden bearer". I am now a sufferer. A cross now lies across my shoulders and it may be there for a long time. It may be months or even years before I can set it down. I may never be able to set it down.

Now, if my life on earth is the most cherished, most important thing to me, I will have a very hard time accepting all this. This disease has critically wounded my life. That is so unfair. And it is unspeakably tragic…..if it is the case that this life on earth is the most important thing. Thankfully, it is not the most important thing. My destiny lies beyond this temporal life on earth. When I recognize this wonderful truth, hope rises up in me and I start to turn into this new life of affliction. My destiny lies above, in the Kingdom of God, in the presence of Christ, seated at the right hand of the Father in all glory. The apostle Paul puts it like this: "our citizenship is in heaven, from which we eagerly wait for a savior, the Lord Jesus Christ". My final destiny is not found on this broken Earth. This is temporal living, but I was created an eternal being for eternal living. I was created and am destined for eternal life in the presence of Christ in His Kingdom. I am destined for a redeemed body and heart and mind; I am destined to be restored to the man God originally created me to be, mind, body and spirit. This present earth journey is a journey to the eternal.

And then another great truth begins to break in on me. My highest purpose on earth is to glorify God. If that is so, how I do that can be left to God Himself. If He chooses to glorify Himself by giving me a long life of comfort and pleasure, free from suffering and affliction, then I glorify Him and fulfill His purpose. And if He chooses to glorify Himself by setting me apart from ordinary life by sending suffering and hardship my way – so be it. That too glorifies Him and my life has fulfilled its purpose. In either case, I glorify Him and fulfill my life purpose. All is well.

If all this is true – and it is certainly true – then I can now release my old life of leisure and comfort and safety and ease and step into another life, even one that carries suffering and hardship. I can accept my cross and take it into my not-ordinary life. Because, thankfully, this life is temporary. And one day – one day – I will be lifted out of it and transferred to the eternal Kingdom of God where I will take my final rest, where I will abide in unspeakable joy and abiding peace of soul forever. That is my sure destiny. And no amount of suffering can spoil it.

July 3, 2016

9

He Targets My Faith

Once God pulls me into this life of hardship and affliction, I must engage my faith to an unprecedented degree. What I see with my senses – suffering and pain and difficulty – is too harsh to take at face value. And, indeed, it ought not be taken at face value, for God is hiding behind the affliction, at work for His glory and for my ultimate good. That is the uncontested footing of faith. That is the great truth that has endured throughout all ages: God works all things after the counsel of His will, which is shaped by His infinite love for me. All He does is from love and for my ultimate good. And in the midst of grief and pain, faith alone can hold that truth.

So, affliction and hardship always have as their aim the expansion and strengthening of my faith. They are divine agents sent to achieve eternal aims. Knowing that the greatest treasure for the believer on earth is his relationship with God through Christ and knowing that that relationship is realized only by faith, God sets out to strengthen and grow my faith by whatever means necessary. And the most sure and powerful of those means is suffering.

God's ways are unfathomable and always aimed at a good that is, quite often, realized far, far into the future. I suspect, more times than not, the aim is a target positioned outside this temporal life in eternity, a benefit I will enjoy eternally when I cross over to my eternal home. But that aim is no less necessary, no less real, no less beneficial, and no less treasured than some near-future earthly one.

Of course this is absolute nonsense to modern ears. Any attempt to bring meaning to pain and suffering by an appeal to some after-life eternal benefit of the soul is foolishness and, even worse, cowardice. And if I give in to this irrational urge (so they reason) I risk losing any temporal benefits that may emerge out of my suffering. I squander, in their eyes, whatever life I still possess. Modern man implores me to accept my suffering – indeed, the very crushing of my life, if need be – for what it is: a tragic, meaningless, empty accident. Confront the whole affair head on, he would implore, standing strong, refusing to give into the siren song of eternal meaning. There is no eternal meaning and, therefore, all one can do is endure suffering and seek to create, out of midair, some temporal meaning around it.

But thank God the eternal does exist. I am an eternal soul and the meaning that is embedded in my suffering is eternal. I suffer to bring glory to God eternally and to grow my eternal soul in preparation for unfathomable joy and everlasting life in His presence. That is enduring meaning, the kind of meaning that stands, unbuckled, under the heavy weight of pain and suffering and hardship so often encountered in this life.

July 3, 2016

10

Life as Gift

Through this affliction I have come to realize I hold a presumption that life is a commodity due me. I harbor a belief that I somehow have a claim on God and He is obliged to keep me living, to keep me living in comfort, and to keep me living for a long time. This is due me.

How absurd. I live at God's good pleasure. My life is a gift from God. And should He snuff out my life today, how could I possibly object? Each day I awake and breathe fresh air is a testimony to God's goodness. He wills it so.

The notion I have some claim to life undermines my struggle to achieve suffering. For if I hold that life is owed me, I have every right to take offense when it is taken from me or spoiled. In that case, to spoil this most precious and deserved commodity is a terrible offense, unjustified, and I have every right to object strongly.

But God determines all the conditions of my life, including length of days. Once I recognize I walk this earth according to the number of days God ordains me to walk, I find a measure of peace when it comes to suffering. When I recognize God's absolute sovereignty over my life, if He takes me home tomorrow, or calls a friend or loved one home, I can surrender to His will and praise Him. I know it is His call, not mine. And I can trust Him that His ways, though mysterious, are perfect. He acts always out of love for me and for my ultimate good. If my life or the life of a loved one is "cut short", I need not despair. Life has not been "cut short". On the contrary, it is simply the case that I did not expect for me or my loved one to depart this earth at this time, yet this is what God had planned all along. There is no such thing as a life cut short. Not knowing God's mind and will, we have an expectation that every life should have a standard number of days on this earth. We call it "average life span". So, if I don't reach my average life span, if I go to be with the Lord years or even decades before I reach it, then it is seen as a life cut short. But that simply is not true. God does not love populations. He loves individual persons. And He has a will for each person regarding the duration of their life on earth. No one has ever died prematurely. God stands sovereign over the life and death of each one of His children.

If this is so, how do we understand the death of the innocent at the hands of the wicked? How do we understand murder? I don't have that answer, except to say this: that men act out of sin is no surprise to God and somehow, in His infinite wisdom, He remains sovereign even over the evil men visit upon other men. It still holds true that lives are not cut short contrary to the sovereign will of God. Nothing takes Him by surprise. Nothing comes about but that He is in total control. He causes or allows all things. Nothing transpires on earth outside His sovereign, total reign. And the great thing is all things – especially the evil that is visited upon His children by wicked men – are redeemed and made right in the end. All things.

July 4, 2016

11

Breakable

Through this hardship I now understand that affliction and suffering are allowed by God for many purposes, most of which are unfathomable, residing in the deep well of His infinite wisdom. Some purposes, however, are apparent, or at least so it seems to me. I now understand that God often uses suffering to break me.

This is hard to take in because it is so counterintuitive to my small mind. What could possibly be gained by breaking me? Actually, it turns out, there is quite a bit of spiritual upside to it.

It is through my weakness that God actually strengthens me, for weakness forces me to abandon my own resources and reach for Him. Brought to the end of myself, I reach the point of personal brokenness, of personal emptiness, and God has an opening to replace my dependence on my own abilities and power with dependence on His abilities and power. Suffering is His tool of choice to achieve that end.

This is a totally different orientation toward life than I see out in the world, which is oriented around the self and personal power. This way – God's way – is different. Through suffering He opens me up to receive infinite power from on high. I hook into the divine source of all strength which is the only source that can carry me into the quality of life God has for me. Left to my powers, I am limited and my ceiling on life is much too low. On the other side of brokenness, I must – and I mean MUST – lean on God. And when I do, immediately my life ceiling lifts and I step into a life that truly has no limits. All is possible because God is "able to do exceeding abundantly" beyond any imagining. I now can live a life that draws power from the Spirit of God alive in me. I release my meager personal power and take hold of the infinite power of God. Now, I step into life accessing a divine power supply and self-imposed limits begin falling away. The hard truth is I cannot possibly get to this point without, somewhere along the way, God breaking me.

I am in good company, for Jesus experienced being broken. He begins his ministry by retreating into the desert for 40 days to fast and be tempted by the devil. And it is the Holy Spirit that leads him into the desert. Is this not a divinely-orchestrated suffering, an intentional breaking of Jesus by the Father? Could it be that Jesus, in his humanity, needed to be broken in much the same way I need to be? Could it be it was this suffering, this breaking of His humanity, that allowed Him to access the full power of the Spirit in Him? Certainly it must be true for me all the more. In order to bring His full power to bear on and within me, God has to empty my flesh. Once emptied, He now can pour in His power, wisdom, and love. As long as I stay filled with my own powers and abilities – that is to say with my flesh – there is no room, there are no internal voids, no gaps, into which God can pour His power. It is in the power of this desert experience of brokenness at the hands of the Father that Jesus steps into his mission on Earth.

Could this be some of what God saw in Joseph that prompted Him to set Him aside as His agent to execute His grand plan for Jacob and his sons? Joseph was willing to be broken. I think that may be what God saw and highly valued in him: he was willing to lose his life. He was malleable enough that God could put him through fire and bring him to the end of himself, confident that Joseph, through his hardships, would faithfully turn to Him for mercy and allow Him to change him. In Joseph He had a man who was willing to lose himself to God and stand open to being changed on the deep level of soul and spirit. He was not so stubborn as to resist God breaking him through suffering.

Could it be God saw this same quality in David – a willingness to be broken? Is this quality, at least in part, what earned David divine praise as a "man after my own heart"? In the Psalms I discover a man who, time and time again, appears to be at the end of himself, wounded and broken, yet relentlessly reaching for God and God's strength.

I finally understand this. This is true humility, the greatest of all humilities: the willingness to be brought to the end of myself at the hands of God, to turn away from my own powers and abilities and live, instead, out of God's power. I am talking about a willingness to lose myself, a willingness to walk away from my ego that must assert itself, that must be affirmed and exalted. I am talking about an openness to die to self and trust God to resurrect me to new life as He will. This is underneath Paul's declaration to the Galatians: "I have been crucified with Christ. And it is no longer I who live, but Christ lives in me. And the life which I now live in the flesh I live by faith in the Son of God who loved me and delivered Himself up for me." Paul died to self – which is the ultimate brokenness – that he might rise again to a new life, a life shaped by the great Potter Himself.

Suffering is the most effective and efficient instrument God has for breaking me. It is painful and hard and I don't like it. I don't want it. But God knows I need it. So, He allows me to suffer that I might break. I finally understand this because I have suffered and been emptied on a deep level and I get it. He broke me. And now, He can make me truly whole, truly powerful…truly me.

July 9, 2018

12

Wants

Suffering immediately separated me from my bag of wants, that, before the affliction, was very important to me. So much of life in America is driven by wants. We think our life will collapse if we are denied them. Yet, if we let God work His eternal purpose in us in our suffering, we quickly recognize that wants, far from making life rich and rewarding, are actually slave masters, burdens, stifling urges that blunt our experience of life.

We suffer under the cultural lie that wants are a pathway to fulfillment. And how terribly misguided this is. Wants are fool's gold – they glitter and get our attention but turn out to be of little value. I really want that new car and am so persuaded that once I get it, I will experience life as rich and full and rewarding. And, of course, at first I do experience a level of satisfaction with the now-fulfilled want – it is so much nicer than the old vehicle. The steering wheel is tighter and the interior is unmarred. But without exception, over time, and often sooner than I would have guessed, the satisfaction wears off and I am left with the same holes in my soul I had before I bought the car. That's because the satisfaction is psychological and emotional, but not spiritual. And only a spiritual patch can patch up my soul.

Suffering and hardship serve to drive wants out of my life. They shine a harsh, blinding light on them, exposing them as imposters that promise fulfillment and satisfaction, but, when it is all said and done, leave me hollow and empty. Suffering compels me to release my wants and hand them over to Christ, lay them at His feet. He alone can fill me up, He alone can fill my soul with what it really needs – love, peace, and joy: in a word, Him.

When our hardship came on us, it stripped away nearly every want I had. Immediately. Like magic, they all fell off, almost as if I simply threw them out onto the street and walked away. Before the hardship, I was a walking collection of wants and a good portion of my waking hours was devoted to strategizing how I might go about satisfying those wants. And I suspect I am not unique in this. But once suffering came along, those things that captured my attention and stirred my desires lost all their luster and were completely incapable of arousing my affections as before.

The experience was at first distressing, and then became, quite unexpectedly, freeing. I was set free from most wants. How strange. That new car, that next-generation high tech gadget or piece of musical gear – they simply lost their pull on me. They lost their potency and were no longer able to arouse my affections. Before Laura's diagnosis, wants shouted loudly in my world. Now, they have fallen silent. Now all that matters is getting her healthy.

This affliction is purifying, wiping away the superfluous, tyrannical wants in my life and bringing me to what is really important and meaningful. I wish I didn't have to go through the fire to get there. It is a harsh, demanding journey. But it has left me in a very good place where trivial wants have been purged and the essentials of life that feed my soul – Christ and Laura and the loved ones in my life – have moved in to take their place.

July 10, 2016

13

My Best Life and True Home

If I see my life on Earth as most important, my primary and best life, I am weak and unsteady. But if I reorient myself and elevate the Kingdom of God above this life, recognizing it as my true home and best life, I am strong and sure-footed.

As a believer in Christ, my true home is not this current Earth. My true home is the future Kingdom of God, and that wonderful truth can steal me in the midst of suffering. The Kingdom is the great end point, the great consummation of life. It is the promise of the Kingdom that assures me that God's works, including suffering, and hardship, and pain, and loss, all have an end point, a purpose that, though unseen, is there nonetheless and will be fully revealed someday. In the Kingdom I will finally reap the eternal benefits of my pain.

The notion that hardship and affliction have an eternal payoff is hard to get my mind around. That's because it has to do with God's grand plan which is too enormous for me to comprehend. I'm like an ant crawling on the back of an elephant. I can only see the smallest portion of God's great work on Earth and cannot begin to understand the role suffering plays. Nevertheless, someday all now mysterious will be revealed.

Of course, His Kingdom is not just a future hope. It is present with me at this very moment in spiritual form and, in a sense, I do not have to wait until I die to enter it. Christ, the great King, is with me throughout my life and in relationship with Him I experience the Kingdom. The full and final expression of the kingdom, however, will not reveal itself until after my death or Christ comes again. Then I take full possession of it and all disappointment, pain and grief are done away and only joy and glory and peace abide.

The Kingdom holds out the great promise of rest from my toil on Earth. Just as Christ sat down at the right hand of the Father after he rose, we too will take our rest in His presence in His Kingdom. From within its borders my struggles and hardships are gone. God's provision is total. The abundance that abides in His fullness spills out into all creation for all His children to receive. The daily grind of living is over and the riches of the glory of His inheritance fall on me like rain.

This is my sure destiny. It is certain. Nothing and no one can take it from me. No matter what I suffer, suffering does not have the final say. No matter what afflictions I encounter, they do not win the day. God has the final say and that final expression is His eternal Kingdom. Suffering will cease and, what's more, the hidden purposes behind the suffering will come to light to the glory of God and our great eternal benefit.

Before Laura's diagnosis I thought life would always be comfortable and fun and easy and nothing could take that away from me. I was living the good life and I was convinced that's the way it should be and would be. That was my right, what was due me. I deserved the good life, a carefree, comfortable existence.

I was wrong. I now see – and I mean really, deeply see – that life is shaky and uncertain and at any moment it can be taken away, changed forever. This life on Earth is not the good life. It is too dangerous to be that. My true home is not this decaying world. I am in exile here. My highest life is not lived out on this Earth – indeed, it cannot possibly be lived out on this Earth with its decay and corruption. My true good life is yet ahead when I go to be with Christ. My true home will one day be revealed when He brings in the Kingdom of God on Earth and restores all creation to its original intended state, free from sin and all sin generates – disease, degradation, tragedy, violence, death. Then, and only then, in the Kingdom of God, will I finally be home and enjoy "the good life": no decay, no disease, no violence, no pain, no tears, no death. Safe and blessed in Him for all eternity, I will finally enjoy the life I have longed for all the days during my stay on this Earth. And it will never be taken away.

July 18, 2016

14

No Rights

This struggle has brought to light a great truth that, before this, troubled me, but now is strangely comforting and empowering: I have no rights to anything in my world. I have no rights to Laura. I have no rights to loved ones and friends. I have no rights to the conditions of my life. All belongs to God to do with as He will. The moment I reach to wrestle my rights back from Him, I set my feet on shifting sand.

The purpose of every life spent on earth is to glorify God. And how that life glorifies Him is totally in His hands. It is His call. If He chooses to glorify himself by allowing me or a loved one to suffer, then so be it. Who am I, the clay, to challenge the potter on anything? He acts in infinite wisdom and power from a heart of infinite love. His ways lie deep within Him. How can I possibly totally understand them?

Still, this is a hard truth to come to. My knee-jerk reaction is to push back on it. For if my life is characterized by hardship and suffering and affliction – how is that fair? How can a loving God will that and still claim to be loving? I think I now have some limited understanding around all this, an understanding forged in fire.

I see now that this life on earth is not the main attraction, but rather the warm-up act. The main attraction, the main event, is eternal life with Christ before the Father in the Kingdom. This temporal life on Earth is a tear drop in the ocean, a blade of grass that grows up for a season and then withers away. Compared to eternity in the Kingdom it is as nothing at all.

But there is still more to it. This temporal life is intended to serve (for lack of a better word) my eternal life. Somehow what I do with this life redounds to my benefit or detriment in the Kingdom. Somehow – and I do not pretend to know exactly how – my suffering enhances my experience of God and glory in the hereafter. Suffering is always redeemed to my good. Sometimes that redemption is partially realized on earth and sometimes that redemption is realized only in heaven and, finally, in the Kingdom. But I will experience the benefit of suffering eventually in either scenario and will enjoy its fruits through eternity. God does not allow His children to suffer for nothing. My suffering bears fruit eternally somehow.

His perfect will works all things together for my good, yes, whether on earth or in glory. But more importantly, He works all things for His ultimate glory. If this is true, then I have no right to demand God act differently in my life. All things exist to glorify Him, which means He is perfectly just and good to "use" all things for that purpose as He will. Whatever the case in my life, whether hardship or comfort, if God is glorified by it, then I have fulfilled the highest purpose for which I was created and for which God sustains me – that is, to glorify Him in all ways.

I have no right to demand God keep His hands off my life. I have no right to demand He keep His hands off my loved ones, my wife, my finances, my career. He has all rights to His creation and to my life. My charge is to seek first His kingdom and His righteous and to love Him with all my heart, soul, mind, and strength. There must be nothing in me above my devotion and love for God. Only then am I in phase with the purpose of God and only then will I live my highest life, a life of joy and peace in faith.

August 9, 2016

15

Cut Off From Tomorrow

This suffering cuts me off from the life activity of planning out my tomorrows. I am suddenly forced into the present, prevented from looking into the future as I normally do. Business plans, vacations, trips, parties, family get togethers: before Laura's diagnosis, crafting these future activities occupied a good portion of my waking hours. Afterwards, they fall off the radar screen altogether. I have no room for them. Living in the hardship is so demanding on my emotional and spiritual energy reserves that I have little left for extraneous matters. These future issues typically bubble up from my inner reservoir of emotional well-being. But this struggle is so emotionally demanding that it leaves me spent down there by the hour. Rare moments of relief are invested in replenishing my reserves, the very time I used to invest in pleasant day dreaming and happy "what-if-ing."

This upheaval I am in squashes inner enthusiasm. So, it is not the case that I would prefer to spend my energy and time planning those more enjoyable matters of life, but begrudgingly have to divert them to the suffering. Rather, it is simply the case that these matters do not even emerge from my heart. They don't bubble up at all. Why? Because they are no longer in my heart. They have left me. I have no space in there for such matters. This affliction has all my attention. Future plans require calm conditions to take shape, but I am in tumultuous weather. The winds and wave of suffering and hardship keep future plans off shore.

If God is all-wise and behind all this, then it must be the case that, for the moment, He wants me to wave off the habit of "future planning" and stay in the here and now. He has some work He wants to perform in my soul, in my heart, in my mind, that can only occur if my attention is unwaveringly set on the present. He intentionally cuts me off from the future for the very purpose of accomplishing this unique work.

And the work must be very important for Him to put me through this pain. It is hard on God to let me suffer. He loves me with an immeasurably deep love. It pains Him when I am in pain. He aches for me and hurts with me. But He allows it, for in His infinite wisdom He has an aim for my life for which He is shooting that is so important to Him and so valuable for me that He is willing to cut me off from the future to achieve it. He knows that with my whole heart and mind stayed on the present, He has my undivided attention. From that place of "now" his work is swift and efficient. He is actually able to compress the pain into a smaller time frame and achieve a greater effect. It is suffering that lets Him achieve that.

In the midst of the darkness, I find hope in Him. I am bound up in the present in suffering. But one day, according to His wisdom, by His love and power, I know He will open the future to me again.

The clouds will finally part and sunlight will shine down and the pain will be taken away. For now, He wants me standing on the rock that is Him, in this suffering, in the present.

August 15, 2016

16

Peace

The only peace I find in this suffering is the peace of abandonment to divine providence. In suffering I come to realize just how much I rely on my experience in the world to give me peace. I trust in calm circumstances, both now and projecting into the future, and I do that without realizing it – it is below my awareness, just the way I navigate my world. As long as my seas are calm – no health problems, no loss, no major disruptions – I experience relative calm.

But calm is not the same as peace. Calm is a product of my environment. I am calm so long as my life conditions are favorable. But stir the waters in my world and I experience emotional upheaval. Peace, by contrast, is an inner state that is anchored in the person of Christ, who He is and what He has done for me. This peace stands on the great truth that my destiny is to live in the presence of Christ and His father for all eternity. It is not dependent upon temporal circumstance. This peace can hold in the midst of turmoil and upheaval and storm and struggle because its roots are eternal. I have assurance that the hardships I experience will not last and that one day this trek on Earth will be over and I will come to rest in the eternal Kingdom of God. Now, turmoil, in the hands of Christ, can actually reinforce that great truth and strengthen my inner experience of peace, stealing me against the vicissitudes of life.

For the believer, adversity brings eternal benefit. It forces me to step off the shaky ground of life conditions and step onto the immovable rock of Christ for my foundation. The more difficult the adversity, the more I am forced to anchor on Him. With my world collapsing, I turn to Him as the only thing left that is solid. All else has, temporarily or permanently, been taken from me. I am left with nothing except Him. And I learn the wonderful truth that He is enough.

And that truth is my rock, my foundation of peace. To the extent I reach for things of this world to stabilize me, I am vulnerable. I can be tripped up by disease or financial struggle or the collapse of a relationship. I can be slammed to earth by tragedy or accident or disaster. When my life conditions are shaken, I am shaken as a person. When life falls away, I cannot endure it. I begin to fall apart.

In the midst of hardship, my natural reaction is to change my life condition so I can get back to a better life. I must get back, somehow, to the way things were so I can feel some life in me again. But this hardship is immovable right now. It won't be changed overnight or even in a few months. This is going to be a long, tough slog. So, I have only one option: turn to Christ. I must now look to Him, and only Him, to salvage and save me in the midst of this struggle. My center of gravity must now be Christ and not the conditions of life.

With Christ as the rock under my feet I now find peace replaces calm, even if in small measure. The winds and rain of adversity still slam up against me as I walk through this storm, but I need not falter. My rock holds. My feet do not slip. In fact, the wind and rain actually now *strengthen* my life structure. They drive my piers even deeper into the Rock, into Christ, shoring me up all the more. Now, I am in a cycle of strength in which storms rage and my foundation becomes stronger. Whereas, from a "calm" orientation, storms only serve to inflict damage and destruction, they now, from a "peace" orientation, become the agents that God uses to strengthen my faith and heart and show Himself all the more real to me. And this leaves me increasingly resilient, able to face adversity and emerge whole and strong because God, through this storm, is becoming all the more real.

August 16, 2016

17

Living For Something Bigger

Suffering brings me to the end of myself. I let go of this notion that my life is so very important, so momentous, and begin to reach beyond me for God. The truth is my life is a part of the grand purpose of the eternal God in creation. He is moving on the earth and has been moving for thousands and thousands of years to bring about His will, which is the Kingdom of God on earth. I have a role to play in that drama. And God decides what role I am to play. My suffering definitely finds meaning and purpose as I realize that God will use it – and this is really quite an incomprehensible and amazing thing – to bring about His purposes in the world, His purposes for all creation, and His purposes for my life.

Up against the backdrop of that understanding, I see my suffering does not diminish my life. It fulfills it. No suffering comes upon me but that it goes through God to get at me. He governs all, including what hardships I am to face. If this is true, then the sufferings I endure in life are needed for me to fulfill all God's great purposes. If they are not needed, then God is sadistic, inflicting pain on me for no purpose. But God infinitely loves me with a love surpassing all understanding. He would never allow me to suffer if that suffering did not advance His sovereign purpose. He intends for me to play a very unique role in His great plan on earth and will not allow me to be derailed from that purpose by suffering or affliction or evil. My responsibility is to humble myself under His mighty, loving hand and trust Him to bring about his perfect will.

In light of this, I must let go of the impulse to live my version of my life and completely abandon my life into His hands that I might live His version of my life. My version will never include suffering and affliction. My version sets me at the center of life. Whatever I see as easy and good for me is what should happen. But it is God who is at the center of all life, including mine. Whatever advances His will and His version of my life is what should happen. When I let go and receive His version of my life, whatever that may be, I find peace and power.

The key for me is to know the love of God that surpasses all understanding. If I can hold deep within me a living and experiential knowledge of His infinite love for me, I will be able to receive whatever He brings into my life, including suffering.

Suffering and affliction feel as if they are spoilers. But I must remember that God is all-wise, all- powerful and all-loving. When all is complete and I cross over to be with Him in glory, I will praise Him, even for the hardships, for I will know that all He allowed, even hardship – or should I say "especially hardship" – advanced His great purposes for my life.

August 23, 2016

18

Faith into Darkness

There are times in the midst of suffering and pain that my faith seems to descend into darkness. I search for God in vain – He is not to be found. That is not to say He is not there. He is. But He has covered Himself in darkness for some divine reason and I am unable to lay hold of Him.

This usually pushes me down the path of despondency. My affliction, as if it is not tough enough, becomes enveloped in darkness. I am dark inside emotionally, unable to see the slightest light in what is now a very dark tunnel. Thoughts turn negative, almost fatalistic. I am covered in affliction and feel it pressing in all around me. In vain I attempt to reach for God, attempt to muster some faith. But I am unable to do so. I am in the clutches of this darkness.

It is confusing. The ground underneath me has inexplicably given way. Through it all, so far, God has been my foothold and I have drawn on His strength to carry me in all this. Now, I am without

Him, flailing in mid-air and in darkness. The only prayer I can muster is "God…..God". I hope that will get some traction and bring light into the darkness, but it doesn't. I am all alone in this, or so it feels.

I had visited Austin yesterday to take care of some things – get Rita (dog) transferred to the neighbors, clean the yard of dog "bombs", pick up the Tribute from Pep Boys (new fuel pump…). Returning to the hospital around 5:00, the darkness grips me. Without realizing it, spending time at the house planted a dark seed of longing that quickly sprouted into despairing. I don't know why and it was completely unexpected. I had visited Austin before, several times over the last 10 weeks, and experienced nothing like this. But today, I had a strong feeling that it would be "forever" before we would ever get back to our home and something resembling a normal life. We had been stripped, it seemed to me, of all we had of our prior life and the overwhelming feeling descended on me that I would never get it back. It felt like death descending upon me, powerfully, irresistibly. The feeling was so strong that, at one fleeting moment, I was on the edge of a panic attack, which, thankfully, did not materialize.

I could not shake the belief that Laura was not making any progress with the Graft-Versus-Host (GVH) disease that had gripped her. She was not advancing – at least that's how it seemed to me. And, in some ways, I thought she was going backwards. The doctors were starting IV nutrition that night, known as TPN. This struck me as a pretty drastic measure and signaled to me that the grip of the GVH was tightening. It was too much. Scenarios swirled in my mind of the worst case – months in the hospital, Laura deteriorating, weakening, the GVH refusing to give way. I imagined Laura developing life-long debilitating complications that would spoil her life into the future. Or, even worse, I feared she would die.

All of this was all too real to me and I couldn't muster the energy to throw it off. It was too heavy. When I did try and push back, it was in the form of that most basic of prayers: "God!....God!"

Through the night Laura was up every 30 – 40 minutes to use the bathroom. And I was up with her, escorting her. She took two insulin shots each night – the IV nutrition had caused her blood sugar to spike. The dark clung to me, thick, oily, heavy. I could not shake it and it ground me down. My imagination was uncontrollable, descending me into ever-darkening predictions of what the future held for her, for us.

Then, God finally breaks through. It comes with a simple word from the doctor the next morning: "She is doing very well. She is making progress." And the Physician's Assistant explains the TPN decision: "Her albumen is low and we want to support that. This is the weakest TPN available, and we are only giving it to her overnight, not round-the-clock. We will discontinue once the GVH settles down. This is not a drastic measure." And, like that, I feel the darkness lift and light comes into the room. I feel an in-swelling of hope and faith. I am revived. The python finally loosens its grip. The ground beneath my feet solidifies. I reach for God...and He is there!

I feel the veil lifting from my mind. Hours clouded in darkness, the shadowed mind is gone, now bathed in light, and I can think straight. Dull eyes suddenly brighten and see again. God has come down and peeled away the darkness. I see Him again.

Scripture floods my thoughts: "For I know the plans I have for you," declares the Lord. "Plans for welfare and not for calamity, to give you a future and a hope." I don't search for it; it simply material-izes in my heart and rings in my ears sweetly. Faith has returned. It is as if I am a bird caught in an uplift of hot air. The darkness flees and the eternal light of God floods in and I am alive, in touch with God, taking in spiritual nutrients once again.

I know this darkness experience is not unique to me. Paul shares his own such experience. He reports that, at some point in his work, he confronts a hardship that leaves him "burdened excessively beyond our strength so that we despaired even of life. Indeed, we had the sentence of death within ourselves..." He is despondent, possibly even suicidal. At the very least Paul's hardship is so intense that he believes he will die. That is darkness. That is despairing. I now know something of that darkness.

Saint after saint writes, through the ages, of this experience of darkness in which God flees, leaving them groping in vain for His presence and comfort. It strikes the modern Christian mind as absurd, unimaginable. God would never do that, they object. But I think He does do that. At times I think He hides away, causing us to desperately reach for Him all the more. God does employ suffering to deepen us into Him, to bring us into a more real experience of Him. And this retreat on the part of God – which is a real suffering for us – purifies us: it is pure faith that must reach for Him because only faith, at that moment, can find Him.

From within the darkness, my faith reaches out again and again. This strengthens it, much like a weight lifter, over-taxing his muscles, builds muscle mass. In the darkness our spiritual eyes have to strain with all their might to see God and they sharpen, bulk up. In the darkness our desire for Him heightens. It swells like a rain-swollen river over spilling its banks. We are consumed with His absence which leaves our heart receptive to the slightest movements of His spirit. From within this strain He strengthens and clarifies and, at the proper time, breaks through to us. Without this "gap" of darkness, God has no opening to do His deepening work in us. A surgeon has to cut us open to repair our insides. God has to as well. He cuts us open by withdrawing from us. And the fortunate result, in time, is a faith that is alive and vital and an experience of the person of God that is deeper, more real, and more durable than ever.

August 27, 2016

19

Duties in the Moment

In the midst of suffering, it helps to orient each day around the simplicity of fulfilling my duty to God for the moment. Since life shrinks up and the future is in some manner snatched away from me, I find purpose and meaning in doing whatever God has for me to do today, this moment, however small. This is my simple duty now in life. And if I fulfill it each day, my life is purposeful and meaningful. I serve and obey God. And that is enough for me.

Out there in the world I have myself convinced my life must embrace so much more than this simple duty to hold any value. It must center around goal and task achievement, whether in work or some other pursuit. And I have to be reaching for the future as well, aiming at something important ahead of me. The more goals I knock off, the more I whittle away at my daily and weekly to-do list, the more I advance into a meaningful future and the better I feel about my life.

And I feel better about me as well. I get a sense of personal worth from all this doing and feel good about "me". This is the main reason I constantly reach for achievement out in the world. I want to feel good about "me". I want to see "me" as a worthy and significant person.

This explains, in part, why the process of shrinking up from daily life, which is inevitable with suffering and affliction, can be so terribly painful – painful on a very deep, personal level: It assaults my sense of self-worth, slapping me in the face, stealing from me the very things I lean on to feel good about who I am in the world.

I find I have two choices at this point. I can emotionally refuse to accept this "stealing away" and stubbornly hold out for that day in the hopefully-not-too-distant future when I finally get back to my life as I knew it, my busyness. If it happens that I get through my affliction quickly and can return to my task-focused life, I will be fine. Of course, I won't grow spiritually or strengthen, but I will be fine. If, on the other hand, my affliction is drawn out, I will soon grow very frustrated and, over time, that frustration will want to morph into disillusionment and bitterness. I can't put my sense of worth "on hold" for months or, even worse, years and maintain emotional wellness. I will feel I am wasting my days, that my life is dead, stagnant, that I am nearly worthless. I cannot endure that for long. That will grind me down and inevitably sink me into depression.

If, on the other hand, I accept this "stealing away" of my life and focus on my duties in the present moment before God, however small they seem, I step onto rich spiritual soil. This is simplicity of a high order. I strip away all fluff of daily life, the busyness that has become my daily routine, and am left with large gaps of time previously filled up with what really amounted to fidgeting, if the truth be told. In my affliction God calls me to fill up those large gaps with small things that seem too unimportant and trivial. But they are actually far from that. These small duties are from God and as I wipe away all else and faithfully, in humility, let them be enough for now, I strengthen into God.

The truth is busyness has no relationship to personal worth and significance. God does not value me based on a score card of accomplishment. I accomplish all I set out to do in a day, and God looks down and says "well done"? No, not at all. That helps me feel good about myself because that is the cultural narrative: personal worth is directly related to productivity. But that is cultural, not divine.

The surprising truth is it is faithfulness to God with the small duties of the day that pleases the Almighty. When I identify what God would have me do today, however minor that may be in my eyes, and set about obeying Him in that, I honor God and serve him. It is a humble offering of "me" in the moment to God. I let go of my view of what is important and humbly accept from God His view of what is important. It is a pure act of losing my life in order to gain my life. For the small, humble duty feels trivial, unimportant and – I say this to my shame – below me, unworthy of me. I am bigger, more important than that. Yet, who am I to decide what is important and what is not? That is God's call, not mine. If God calls me to the most trivial and menial task for the day, and nothing more, then so be it. All callings of God are important! In achieving that menial task, I obey God and fulfill His will for me for the moment. That is terribly important. What more can I ask of life? To look back on the day and be able to say "I did what God asked of me today" – well, that is everything. There is nothing more to add to that.

And it turns out that is more than enough. To faithfully, unto God, fulfill the duty He has placed on me for the moment, irrelevant of its size or worth in my or anyone else's eyes, is to take hold of the pure essence of purpose in life, the very root of purpose in life. It is an act of humble devotion to God and there is absolutely nothing in it for me in the way of praise from men or self-advancement. I do not become big in the eyes of men by humbly helping my wife to the shower, by heating up a bowl of soup for her for lunch, by sitting by her as she sleeps; I am not counted among the ranks of great men simply by praying for her throughout the day, by reading her passages of scripture at night before we turn in, by gently stroking her hair when she is afraid. It is no great achievement in the eyes of others to get up in the middle of the night to help her to the bathroom or pull the covers over her when she returns to bed. These are trivial things in the eyes of men. But these are the great things of God.

August 29, 2016

20

Nothing Left Of Me

Because of this hardship we are going through, my approach to life has shifted. My aim now is to live a life such that, outside of what God fills up, there is nothing left of me. I am totally filled up with Him.

Affliction and suffering promote this way of living because they threaten to take away that which is so important to me: Laura. I confront the possibility of living without her and I come to realize how unimportant the rest of all this living really is.

So, if that is the case, then what really makes life meaningful and worthwhile? And the uncontested answer is "a relationship with God". I simply could not find anything else that could step in and fill the void that she would leave behind. All possible fillers proved hollow: music, therapy, writing, building. All wilted under the hot, scorching sun of being alone in the world without her.

That got my attention. If I hope to live a life of power and purpose, I must live life from a meaning posture that can withstand absolutely anything that can be thrown at it. It is no worthwhile life-view that collapses the moment life gets truly difficult, the moment life rips from me something of great worth. Such a guiding life-view is a feckless weakling. And I found that, without knowing it, I was placing a lot of stock in these "things" of my life to give me meaning and, more specifically, a feeling of self-worth and purpose.

This revealed to me that my relationship with God was holding second place to these things. I was really holding my various pursuits or successes or achievements or life ambitions as pre-eminent in my life. To be sure, God definitely had a place along with these other things – I was not leaving Him out of the mix. But the threat of losing Laura quickly uncovered the reality that He was not my sole foundation and life footing.

I was looking to my life to fill me up and make life meaningful. That's it. I didn't even realize it. In fact, I really thought I was supposed to do exactly that: I was supposed to craft such a life that it filled me up and conferred on me value and self-worth and significance. Yes. I thought the aim in life was to put together an exceptional and amazing life. Having done that, I would achieve a meaningful life and become a worthwhile man.

This had to be corrected and quickly. The whole of what I actually did value – not what I told myself I valued – was unable to stand up under the crushing weight of Laura's diagnosis. I was left frightened and desperate. Thankfully, and by His grace, it did not take me long to throw all the things aside and flee to God. I had no choice. I was going under.

I discovered God in a brand-new way. He is not a companion God, not a God who plays a supporting role in my life, not a God who lends a helping hand here and there. Rather, He is my God who is the absolute anchor of my soul, the singular foundation of my very life, the only hope and confidence available to me in this world. A yearning rose up in me that He swallow me up in His great person and take the uncontested and unchallenged position of pre-eminence. I wanted only Him because I finally came to understand, through suffering, that all other ground is sinking sand. I longed to have Him take possession of me, all of me so that, outside of what He has of me, there is nothing left of me.

September 4, 2016

21

Emptying

In the midst of suffering, it often seems to me that there is no end to it. It just keeps pressing down on me relentlessly. I strap myself in and endure and endure, periodically looking ahead to see if there might be a faint ray of light ahead. But it doesn't show. So, I pull the strap tighter and carry on, eyes searching the horizon for some light. I see nothing but darkness. It's as if I am falling and there is no solid ground below, only empty space. I fear I will just keep falling and never stop.

Many a time I felt I had reached my limit and just couldn't endure much more of this. This was more common, however, on the front end of the trial. As I walked deeper into the affliction, through prayer and seeking God, those moments diminished in frequency.

What accounts for this? How was it those "can't-go-on" diminished in frequency? Well, it must be I am increasing in strength, having been stretched and tested over time. This testing has increased my endurance.

No, that is not exactly what I experienced. I think I came into a deep spiritual experience of losing my life to God. Somewhere along the way, somehow, I stepped into a breaking of me, a dramatic emptying of me. The unrelenting, protracted pressure of the suffering was breaking me down and emptying me of personal strength. One would expect it would have the opposite effect and I would experience an increase, over time, of inner power. But that is not what happened. My inner reserves were being depleted, not replenished. My personal power was waning, not reviving.

And that had to happen. I now understand that I cannot really strengthen until I reach total weakness. I cannot really be filled up spiritually until I am totally emptied. God can fill a vessel only if it is empty. This is what affliction and suffering do: they empty completely; they break down, they destroy, they use up and deplete my natural powers (as frail and brittle as they are) so that divine power might find on empty receptacle into which it can be poured.

The power of God in me does not augment my natural powers. It is not as if God takes my natural powers and makes them a little stronger with His power. No, His power must be all power in me if I am to live a life of true power. The divine is not a supplement to the natural. The divine must be all in all. He employs suffering as the agent to bring about a complete breaking and emptying. Then, at that point, affliction is withdrawn and He begins to rebuild and fill.

The suffering does not endure forever, only long enough to deplete me. Saints in all ages hold on to the comfort that, at some point, the pain will be over and we will enjoy peace and great joy on into eternity. The pain of night will end up in our rear view mirror, reduced to a memory that grows unrelentingly faint. But the joy of morning will eternally increase, filling me to a fullness never known.

September 7, 2016

22

Inside World of Soul

This suffering is forcing me to come to an essential understanding about life: abundant life must first be lived from the inside world of soul, then extended to the outside world of flesh.

The footing of this life is eternal soul. I am an eternal soul. That is the essence of me, the part of me that endures and is constant, year in and year out. My physical body is the fruit of this soul, which is the seed. Soul is the DNA, if you will, of my body and my life.

The world inevitably draws me into an orientation that sees life as merely an outward pursuit. I become distracted and supremely concerned about extending my reach out into the world around me and making something happen or taking something in. Life is about what's out there in the world and the actions I take to impact it or receive it.

And that sets me up for failure when I encounter affliction and suffering. For suffering strips me of the outside world of action, as I have known it, and leaves me with only the inside world of soul. If I live only in response to or relation with the outside world of action, I am in a weak and vulnerable space.

For it is the inside world of soul that is called upon to stand up under pain and affliction. Faith lives in the inside world of soul and it is only faith that can reach through the pain and find good and hope and joy and confidence in suffering. All these spiritual realities are there, even in the pain, for God is there, carrying us through all our sufferings into everlasting joy and peace. Faith can hold that truth, remaining open to God's good purpose, however mysterious, while in pain. Flesh simply cannot.

If my inside world of soul is strong, it is of little importance – it certainly is not determinative – what happens in the outside world of flesh. Suffering can so profoundly spoil the circumstances and conditions of my life that I find no comfort from them. Instead, it forces me to stand on soul to find enduring life, to find comfort and peace and hope and solace. With my life crashing in all around me – through pain or death or disease or financial ruin – soul alone can remain strong, the firm footing I need, the anchor that holds. That's because soul is firmly grounded in the eternal, unseen realities of life: I am eternal, never to die and have a sure hope of resurrection to eternal life. I am confident that one day I will be transported from this earth over to paradise, the very presence of the most-high God, there to find unending joy and peace forever. The glory that will finally be revealed to me is so brilliant, words cannot begin to describe it.

And soul becomes my sure refuge in the midst of the storm as well. In pain, my soul reaches for God, knowing He is with me and sovereignly moves in my life for my good and to His glory. He is right in the middle of the storm, riding it out with me. Whatever I face, my soul embraces this blessed truth and I find real, living meaning and hope in the middle of pain and suffering. Flesh is powerless here. It only knows the pain, the depression, the fear; it only sees the wind and the waves crashing against the boat. Soul reaches up to heaven and gazes upon the Father of all glory and power and is reassured that, despite what I see all around, all is well....all will finally be well.

September 11, 2016

23

Losing Life, Losing Fear

At some point into this trial I realized that my feeling of fear had shifted. It seemed to have lost its punch-to-the-gut quality that it has had all my life. Why? The reality of my eternal life in Christ has become more real to me. This temporal life is so very short and passing. That knowledge makes suffering and affliction less momentous than it would otherwise be.

God's sovereignty is unquestioned and total to me now. I used to see life as mostly running independent of God's involvement – a deistic view. It was the only way I could preserve the free will of man and come to understand evil and sin. Now, I see God as absolutely and completely in control of every event and circumstance in life, period. Everything that gets at me – absolutely everything – must go through God first. Nothing gets at me but that He allows it. And if He allows it, it will redound to His glory and my ultimate benefit, whether in this life or the next. He never allows anything to touch me that will diminish my life. All in my life is there by the will of God, an agent for my eternal good and the eternal health and development of my soul.

I have lost my fear in life because I have lost my life, really for the first time. All my life I have had an agenda: to live my version of my life. And I thought nothing of that. That is the way it is supposed to be, or so I believed. A person is supposed to take stock in themselves, identify their strengths and heart desires, identify meaningful goals and dreams, and put all their effort into making all that a reality. All that talk from Jesus about losing my life to save it: I thought that was about holding Him as pre-eminent in my life. I was doing that by virtue of the fact I had received Him as my Lord, my God, my savior. To me, that was losing my life.

But that is not the same as losing my life. I have come to understand that losing my life is coming to a posture of complete and utter abandonment of every aspect of my life to the absolute divine providence of my Father. It is letting go, completely and totally, of living my version of my life and being open, without any reservation whatsoever, to accepting God's version of my life, whatever that entails. And from within such a perspective, I find fear simply has no place to gain any foothold.

Why would that be so hard a posture to take? Because God's version very likely will include suffering and loss. If I am unwilling to accept affliction and suffering from God, I will not be able to abandon myself to divine providence. Fear will remain, as strong as ever. I will be frightened and anxious and will keep my hand on the steering wheel. That is not losing my life. Rather, that is holding onto fear.

Knowing that this life is not my highest life, that it is a prelude to my true and highest life in the kingdom with Christ in the presence of the Father, goes a long way to helping me abandon my life to divine providence and releasing fear. I know my eternal life is sure and someday this temporal existence will be over and I will enter into the kingdom of God where I will have a new imperishable body, inhabit my new mansion, and dwell in a new heaven and new earth in the presence of God forever. That eternal life is my true life. That is what I was created for. This life on earth is merely a warm up act for the main event. That being true, I can accept that suffering and affliction will be part of this life and that is fine.

Before, I was deathly afraid of suffering. I saw it as an unacceptable and abhorrent spoiler of my life. If this life is my highest life, the most important experience out there, then having it spoiled by affliction is immeasurably tragic and unacceptable. But this life is fleeting and my highest life and final destiny lie beyond it. This life serves eternal life and God uses it to mold my soul in preparation for my true eternal life with Him. This is a life of preparation, a training field in which God is transforming me into the image of Christ so that, when He calls me home, I am suited for life in His presence.

Now, that totally shifts my perspective on suffering. I now can see it as a divine agent sent to advance the state of my eternal soul. And that is something I can deal with. That gives it divine and eternal meaning.

Suffering affords me the opportunity to glorify God in ways I could not possibly do apart from it. If I suffer well, in faith, holding to God with everything I have, looking to Him and trusting, as best I can, His love for me even while I suffer, that speaks volumes to the world. Suffering well, I leave behind eternal seeds sprinkled in the lives of the people who have come across me. God uses my suffering to speak to them of His greatness and grace, to speak to them of His faithfulness, to speak to them of His love in that He redeemed me and will redeem me. If others see that I value heaven so much more than this life, that my heart is in heaven, which is my true home; if others see that I understand this life as a journey in a foreign land and that I am looking for my home in in the Kingdom with Christ, they will be deeply touched and challenged. They will not be able to explain that away or dismiss it. An honest, heartfelt cry to God of "Praise you. I am trusting in You" from within my suffering leaves others speechless. Nothing can discredit that. I am, through the suffering, forcefully brought to the reality of the eternal God in my life and they won't be able to deny that. It will penetrate their heart. God uses my suffering to touch deeply the hearts of others who look in on it.

September 13, 2016

24

To His Glory And My Good

God is absolutely sovereign. That means nothing gets to me that doesn't go through Him first. Everything passes through the filter of His wisdom, His purposes.

What a comfort in times of affliction. I do not suffer for nothing. God's will is not capricious nor is it neutral, as though he were on the sidelines, looking on as I struggle, hoping for the best. No, rather, He is four and five steps ahead of me moving things seen and things unseen in divine coordination to bring about His divine will for my life.

And everything He does is for my best. I do not know how, but my suffering not only brings about God's glory but my greatest satisfaction in Him. Sometimes I see the fruits of my suffering on earth and can put two and two together and make sense of it all. Sometimes I must wait until that glorious moment when He calls me to Himself at death. Then, because of my suffering and affliction, my experience of Him is all the greater and my fullness is all the more full.

And it is so full and satisfying on the level of soul that I forget about the suffering and it seems as nothing. This is what Jesus alludes to in John 16 when he tells his disciples their sorrow will be turned to joy. He gives the illustration of a woman in childbirth: "Whenever a woman is in travail she has sorrow, because her hour has come; but when she gives birth to the child, she remembers the anguish no more, for joy that a child has been born into the world." John 16:21. Our joy after suffering is so complete and full that we remember the pain no more. To see him face to face, to be with him finally, so completes and fills us – the experience is unprecedented and unimaginable. We have nothing to even compare to it. The closest we can come is a woman giving birth to a child. Pain gives way to unspeakable and unimaginable joy. And our suffering makes the joy all the more full because of the pain.

Just look at Christ, our great example. He suffered greatly, greater than any man has ever suffered. And He did it for the glory that God had in store for Him. God promised to highly exalt Him on the other side of the suffering, and He did just that. God had to put him through tremendous suffering – His only beloved son – to achieve the ultimate glory He had for him. And it is no different in my life. At times He needs to put me through trials and suffering in order to bring me to the high exalted place He intends me to occupy. Christ's suffering brought him to the glory God had for him. My suffering will, one day, do the same for me for I am in the hands of the same God.

It is a true statement to say that God suffers when I suffer. It pains Him terribly to see me in pain and agony. It cuts His loving heart deeply. He suffers. Yet it is that same deep love for me that moves Him to allow it because He knows the end game – He knows the glory and joy that will be mine on the other side of the suffering and He jealously wants that for me. He is willing to let me endure a temporary affliction that will soon end in order to obtain an eternal benefit that can never be taken away.

October 20, 2016

25

The Clear Eye

Living into hardship and pain and affliction, your eye becomes clear, maybe for the first time. You see under the skin of life into the very marrow of the bone. And what you see is the dark side and harsh reality that life is unsafe and can crush the life out of you at any moment.

You see, as clear as a spot light penetrating the night sky, what is meaningful and what is not. The pursuits and ambitions of your life, so important before your suffering, are suddenly rather insignificant, if not downright unimportant. The loved ones in your life become everything.

On the other side of suffering, once the pain subsides and life becomes "normal" again, you find your eye begins to darken again and you are slipping into seeing life like you used to see it. You might even notice a desire to get back to that "normal" you enjoyed before your affliction. Some may be able to do just that. And that is sad.

Because it means they have learned nothing – they have not been changed, transformed by their ordeal.

Many – maybe even most – will not be able to return. Of those, a fairly large percentage will not recover and will, tragically, live out their life broken and depressed. Or they will turn to some external "comfort" like substance abuse to help them cope with lingering emotional pain. Or they will withdraw from relationships and walk through their world in isolation, simply unable to genuinely engage with loved ones any more.

Yet some of those who find they are unable to return to their former life will walk through the remainder of their life with a clear eye, seeing the true nature of this life on earth: how temporary and unpredictable it is; how each moment of each day is unsafe; how vulnerable they are to death and disease and loss. And this clear-eye vision will, hopefully, force them to look upward toward heaven and reach for God, who alone is our safety and surety. They will, for the remainder of their days, refuse to pour their life into temporal pursuits that ultimately fail and hold no meaning and reorient around the notions of calling and purpose. They will reach for loved ones, friends, and fellow human beings that they might serve them, love them, enjoy them. This is not so much a discipline or inner commitment as it is a compulsion – they have been changed and can do no other.

If you are one of these people, your walk through this life will now be a lonely one in many ways. That's because most of the people you interact with – well, their eye is still dark. They haven't had the blinding-light experience of suffering and pain. They believe the lie that life is about advancing their self-interests and securing pleasure and comfort for themselves. They think they are safe and are convinced that tomorrow will find their world intact and moving along just fine, just like it always has. They won't even really see their loved ones and friends. They will look right past them, like you do a windshield on a car. They are simply fixtures to them, always there, taken for granted. They will appear to be happy – at least happy enough. They will appear to have not a care in the world. They will be achieving and succeeding and taking in life.

But if your eye is clear from suffering, that path is closed to you forever. And thank God that it is. Because you now know that life on earth is temporary and unsafe and the only things that are meaningful and worth your time are God and others and heaven. You see for the first time. You are now walking in the light, living in the truth. Christ said "the light of the body is the eye. If the eye is clear, your whole body will be full of light. But if your eye is bad, your whole body will be full of darkness. If therefore the light that is in you is darkness, how great is the darkness." Now, finally, because of your suffering, your eye is clear....and you get it. Get down on your knees and thank God you do!

October 29, 2016

26

Life As Prelude

In pursuit of losing my life to God, I have to also lose my perception of the nature of this life. This life on earth is not an end in itself. It is prelude, the great aim of which is the kingdom and eternal life with Christ before the Father. That is what I was created for. I was created to enjoy the greatest greatness that exists in the universe, namely, Christ Himself. I was not created for this world. God never intended I live in this flawed world trapped in this fragile, humble body. This current state of creation is fatally flawed and corrupt and will one day pass away. Which means the life I live down here is neither my highest life nor my loftiest hope. It is not an end of itself; rather, it is a passing through, a temporary journey to a greater, enduring, eternal home. I am walking toward eternal life with God. My home is the Kingdom of God. That is my highest life and my sure destiny.

Therefore, I am not to raise this life up on a pedestal and worship it. I am not to approach it as a final destination. Rather, I am to approach it as a temporary journey. I am not to rest in it as my final home; I am to live an exile life, treating this life as a temporary tent, reaching for my true home in the presence of God and Christ, longing to take my rest in God's kingdom. This life is not a resting place. It is a place of toil and effort and fatigue and struggle. It is a temporary and fleeting existence, a brief experience to lead me to eternity. I was made for the eternal Kingdom of God, not this temporal world of earth.

How does this impact my experience of suffering? Once I embrace life as a journey that ends at the throne room of God where I will forever enjoy fellowship with Him, I take a stand on eternal ground. Feet planted on such a solid rock, I am unmoved when temporal ground gives way. It will not take me down with it because my rock holds. My destiny is sure. My home is unshakable. The world around me crumbles, but I stand solid and strong because my soul, the very eternal, enduring essence of "me", is safe in God, invulnerable to the vicissitudes of this life. Thus positioned, I can endure hardship knowing it is temporary and will not win out; knowing that life and love and joy win out. I am destined for eternal peace and rest and gladness in the presence of Christ and His Father. No amount of suffering can change that.

December 30, 2016

27

Relocating Peace and Joy

From within this affliction, it seems peace and joy have fled. And it takes a while for me to understand the reality that is behind what I am feeling. For they have not left me, they have simply been relocated – if I let them be.

This experience of disease has uncovered a glaring, deep weakness in me. All along I have placed joy and peace out there in my circumstances, and up to now that has proven a safe residing place. But this disease has drawn the curtain back on the lie. It was a magician's sleight of hand that tricked me to believe my world is safe and well-ordered and under control and will continue to serve up good things, pleasant things, indefinitely. My blue skies deceived me. Seeming to stretch endlessly into the horizon, they convinced me they would never leave. The occasional storm clouds that did show up always gave way to blue skies. The world felt solid under my feet and the sky ever blue.

But Laura's disease exposed the illusion. Even though Laura continues to improve and recover well from her transplant, I can never again rest in my circumstances and place faith in favorable conditions. The harsh truth has arrived and will not leave: this life, this world, is lethal and I am not protected from the worst it has to offer.

So, my peace and joy can no longer find safe ground in a naïve faith in fortune. It's as if I walked around with my eyes closed and fingers crossed. And when I would get a report of someone getting a cancer diagnosis or hear of someone's child being killed in a car accident or watch the news and see the suffering of people in far-away foreign lands, I would mutter to myself "okay, that wasn't me. My luck still holds. That won't happen to me."

Then it did happen to me. I was the one whose wife got the diagnosis of a terminal disease. I was the one facing the frightening prospect of watching a loved one endure a dangerous, potentially fatal, bone marrow transplant. Fortune failed me.

It takes only one affliction to expose fortune as an unreliable ally. I can no longer – not now and not ever – look for joy and peace out there in the world. Not that it doesn't possess that, don't get me wrong. It simply can't offer any guarantee of it. And for me it is now too risky to leave those most precious commodities in the hands of fortune.

That puts me in a tough spot. I can't live without peace and joy and now I can't depend on them in this world. And this is the great lesson I have learned:

This life cannot hold peace and joy securely for me; only God can. I must now turn from leaning on fortune as a place holder for joy and peace, and place them in His care. And when hardships overwhelm me – and they surely will again – I can rest in the great truth of God: that He is absolutely sovereign over all events in my life. The circumstances of my life are in His hands. Therefore, my destiny is safe and sure. Whatever I face in this life, He is in charge and He will work it for His glory and my ultimate good.

I will suffer in this life. And He will transform my suffering into blessing that will redound to my good through all eternity. He has delivered me from this domain of darkness and transferred me to the Kingdom of His Son. And when death comes for me, He will take my hand and escort me to the gates of that Kingdom. In there I will step into my final joy and peace – a joy and peace incomprehensible to me, everlasting, imperishable. In that moment all suffering will end and I will see, for the first time, the purpose of it all. That is when I will breathe a deep sigh and say "thank you, thank you, thank you, God."

June 14, 2017

28

Touchable

I now seem to carry around an emotional bag that is new to me. Going through my day I notice a different type of anxiety below the surface, the root of which is planted in the reality that I am vulnerable and unsafe. I am touchable.

Before Laura's diagnosis, the notion that terminal disease would touch me was of little concern. I, like most people, would hear of a friend of a friend coming down with some form of cancer and would feel badly for them. The news would bring up an emotional pang of sympathy, even a smidgeon of fear, but these reactions would pass and I would go about my business. It was understood – I understood it – that I was a member of the chosen class of untouchables whose journey in life would include none of the bad stuff that befalls others. The day we learned of Laura's disease was the day I became touchable.

Of course, I have been touchable all along, as is anyone who draws breath on this fallen world. No one walks through this life with a magic bubble around them insulating them from hardship and loss. But until you are actually touched, you hold on to that illusion because you have to. How else could any of us navigate our daily journey? We could not possibly carry around, day in and day out, a heightened sense of vulnerability. It is too heavy a burden, so we adopt the lie of invulnerability.

Being touched by tragedy or disease is not a one-off experience. That is to say, I don't get back to the life I had before I was touched once the tragedy or disease is behind me. When you are touched, the bubble is shattered once and for all. You can never crawl back into your untouchable life and feel all safe and invulnerable again. You will forever walk through the world with a real sense that you are not safe and anything can happen to you.

It is a daunting challenge to live well in this state because you have no place to sit down and rest. You are ever on the alert, to some degree. You can't just kick back and let go like you used to. When I was untouchable, in the bubble, I could often completely let go emotionally without a care in the world and simply enjoy life. Now, it is different. There is an attending low-grade anxiety that leaves me always vigilante, always slightly charged in preparation for the next struggle or hardship life might throw at me.

The question becomes: how do I move forward in this new state of vulnerability? For me, the answer has been spiritual. First, I had to shift my full trust and hope from good fortune out in the world to the eternal God. His infinite love, infinite wisdom and limitless power are my bubble now. This world will throw at me what it may, yet   He remains faithful. He remains my true salvation. I know nothing can touch me but that it gets sifted through His hands. He is absolutely sovereign and He will not allow anything to touch me that will ruin me. No matter what I have to face, God will see to it my life fulfills the purposes for which He created me and see me safely to my eternal home with Him.

Secondly, I had to shift the focus of my life from the conditions of my world and my physical well-being to the condition of my soul and my spiritual well-being. That wonderful old hymn says it so well:

When peace like a river attendeth my way

When sorrows like sea billows roll

Whatever my lot Thou has taught me to say

It is well, it is well with *my soul.*

Yes, that is it. It may not be well with my body. It may not be well with my life - the conditions of my life may be awful. Even so, it is always well with my soul. That is the great secret to living life as one of the "touchables". All is well with my soul, that eternal "me" that endures beyond all time. My soul has been redeemed and restored. My soul remains untouchable, safe and secure from all tragedy or disease. My body may be touched, my life may be touched, but my soul is untouched and untouchable, hidden in Christ who is seated at the right hand of the Father.

No matter what may come upon my life in this world, I now know that all is truly well with my soul. And someday soon my soul will flee to Christ to enter my destiny in His presence before the Father forever. When that day comes, all the tragedy and pain and loss I encounter in this life will be over. It will be gone, finished, done. And forever more I – that eternal soul – will dwell in joy and peace, safe. I will then finally, at last and forever, be untouchable.

June 26, 2017

29

Vertical

Before Laura's diagnosis it is clear that I understood this life as a brief journey on the earth, a horizontal journey, a walk along a flat path. Someday I would come to the end of that path and this horizontal life. At that point, I would jump up on to the next horizontal line, an eternal path, and take my first steps into eternal life in the presence of God.

Without realizing it, my vision of living was of two paths which really amount to two distinct lives: this first life down here on the earth, mortal; the second life up there in heaven, eternal. My understanding has shifted dramatically because of our affliction and no doubt for the better.

Am I living two lives? Of course not. The "me" on earth is the "me" that one day will abide with God and look upon Christ face to face. Christ came to cleanse us of sin and ready us to enter heaven upon death and, eventually, according to the Father's good time, to enter the Kingdom of God on earth. He will lead all who are in Him from this mortal, earthly existence into His eternal Kingdom.

The problem is I was thinking horizontally, not vertically. I was visualizing my walk on earth as a walk along a horizontal plain. But it is not that. In reality it is a walk up an incline, a slow but steady ascension to the infinite. I am not strolling across a flat open field of grass towards a stone wall on the other side. No, I am climbing a long, rocky slope of ground. And as I finish my journey and crest the summit, I will find, not a stone wall, but an immense city laid out before me, covering the entire ground of an endless valley, glittering under a strange and irresistible light, spreading out as far as the eye can see. It is the glorious Kingdom of God – my final destiny!

Then, worn down and dirty from my journey, I will dust myself off and – but what is this? There is no dust to wipe away. My clothes, just moments ago dirty, tattered and thread bare from the journey, are suddenly like new, brilliant in color, so dazzling that they hurt my eyes. And what is this? Everything around me, the gray and brown that marked my path, is suddenly dazzling and alive with color. I have never seen colors so sharp. I have never known vision so clear. In fact, now that I gather myself and look around, the ground itself is strange, its contour more lovely than I ever remember. Ground previously occupied by rock and dirt now teems with grass and trees that shine out a wonderful, colorful glory.

Now I am on new ground and a new journey has begun. No, that is not exactly correct. The ground is new, true, but my journey is not a new one; rather, it continues. It is only the ground that has changed; only the mortal earth phase of my journey that is over.

And this is what I didn't get before our time of suffering arrived. The end of my earth journey is the start of my journey into the infinite, but it is all one journey. It is "me" walking on earth and "me" walking in eternity in the Kingdom. The same me that trudged for so long through the tough slog of this earth will now walk into the eternal Kingdom of God. There is a brand new world before me to explore and enjoy. And there is a King to get to know, a King whose very life is my life, who has lived in eternity past and will live into eternity future. The best portion of my journey has finally begun. All the pain and struggle on earth was prelude, necessary preparation for this glorious moment.

Life is vertical, an ascending. It is not horizontal. From my very first breath at birth I have been on an ascending path to the infinite kingdom. This brief walk on earth accounts for the first phase of my journey. It is by no means the last phase. For I journey toward the glorious destination of the Kingdom of God. And from within the walls of the Kingdom, my journey will continue on. Thank God.

June 30, 2017

30

Not About Learning

Walking through this hardship, I have come to believe God's aim in affliction is not learning. He means to break me that I might, in pain, reach for Him. He doesn't want to give me a lesson on life. He wants to give me Himself. He wants me to know Him more truly and desire Him more desperately.

Each hardship I encounter in this life is potentially redemptive if I allow it to evoke in me a response of reaching out for Him in a desperate bid to touch Him. What could be more beneficial for me? My problem in life is not that I haven't learned what I need to learn – I don't necessarily suffer from a learning deficit. My problem is I really don't believe in Him. I really don't know Him. I really don't trust Him and rest in His absolute sovereignty. I have a God deficit in my life and that's what God seeks to impact when He allows hardship to cross my path.

I don't want to overstate this, if that is indeed possible. There are times when life simply annoys me and I encounter little pests along my path. Like pesky mosquitoes buzzing my face, day-to-day hassles pester me. This is when, I now understand, God would have me to take account of my behavior or my beliefs or my choices as He prods me to stop and reflect and learn something. But when it comes to affliction and suffering, it is simply too shallow an understanding of all this to think that, in those times that crush me to dust, God's grand purpose is to merely change my thinking, to get me to see things differently, to help me understand something and make different choices. In my view that simply doesn't match up with the enormity of the hardship. Under the crushing weight of it, I am confronted with something more than a tame discomfort. I find suffocating desperation and it is that desperation that compels me to reach for God Himself, not some skinny life lesson. At that moment only He will do, nothing less. That is the divine purpose for the affliction.

This is a hard reality, really, in human terms. We are not used to seeing God, the loving father of Christ, as a being who would insert suffering into the life of one of His beloved children. It offends our sensibilities. But this sentiment is horizontal, earth-bound, even if understandable. It presumes that this life on earth is most important and whatever spoils my enjoyment of life or prevents me from living my life to its fullest expression (as many understand that) is an unjustified offense. It can be nothing other than unspeakably tragic. From within such a worldview, my life on earth is everything and no loving God would spoil that.

To my great surprise that was my perspective. And it took Laura's diagnosis to tease it out of me. I was devastated at the thought of Laura going through pain and suffering, having her life possibly diminished and shortened by this disease. It struck me as offensive and terribly unjust.

However, over the next few months, as I desperately, through tears, prayed to God, seeking Him from a depth of heart I had not reached before, my eyes began to open. It became progressively clear that I was trapped in the horizontal, the earth-bound view. I began to see and deeply embrace the truth that this earth portion of my life is temporary and not the highest life I am to experience. It is not my great destiny. Eternal life in the Kingdom of God – that is my destiny. That is my highest life, not this trudging journey on earth. The more that truth took hold of me, the more life flowed back into me.

And now I understand what He wants to achieve in me through this suffering. His aim is not to teach me. His aim is so much higher than that, so much deeper and enduring. He wants me to find Him more completely and rest in Him fully. He wants me to fall head long into the true hope of eternal life in Christ and let that be my rock in this world. From that place of living faith my soul is filled up to overflowing and I am steadied on my path. It is my suffering that has opened my eyes to the great truth that He alone is sovereign and in control of my life, that He alone can bring eternal significance and redemption into every experience of life, whether pleasant or unpleasant. That significance and that redemption are found only in living union with Him.

July 19, 2017

31

Expecting Easy

I was not prepared to suffer. My whole life has been lived in a culture that expects life to be easy, fun. Everywhere I look the pop media throw up images of people – usually young people – having a great time, drinking a beer or eating at some upscale restaurant or driving a new car. They are smiling and laughing and having a party. All this builds a perception in my heart that life is an effortless undertaking. I begin to believe that life is and should be a party, a good time. In the face of this onslaught of happy I inevitably become emotionally inoculated to suffering and difficulty, lacking the emotional antibodies needed to fight off despair when in the throes of life's hardships.

So, when we got the news that something was seriously wrong with Laura, that she had a very serious disease, I struggled mightily. It was like an anvil falling on me from a four-story window. The initial blow was crushing.

I was stunned. It was difficult to believe what I was being told. Suddenly we were in a storm, a raging storm and I was flailing about, fighting off waves of fear and panic. We didn't know yet specifically what disease she was facing, but we knew it was in her bones and that was as bad as it could get. We were looking at a possible death sentence for her, for all we knew. I could lose her in six months, a year. I could be facing the worst imaginable. My fears were racing. Life turned from easy and light to hard and heavy – just like that! The shift was so fast it was difficult for me to make any sense of it. I was in a dull state of fear.

As I look back on those first weeks, I understand that I had fully inculcated the cultural message that life is supposed to be easy. I just knew that bad things, things that crush and grind down people, only happen to others. I believed I was part of the "fortunate club" whose members smile and laugh and enjoy all the great things and experiences that life brings. Affliction never touches them. And what's worse, I believed I deserved just such a life. It was what was due me, and I was confident I would never be deprived of it like those other poor souls fighting disease and tragedy. This was my mindset. And it was exposed and swept away in an instant.

My initial reaction to her diagnosis was complete resistance. No, this cannot happen. This is outrageous, unacceptable. We are not meant to join the crowd of the suffering. We are meant to live an easy life and then die an easy death. Laura is a healthy, vital woman and it is unjust that she has to take her place with the sick and suffering. That was an unbearable thought. I could feel the emotional convulsion within me, churning in my stomach, pushing back at our new reality in my feeble attempt to throw this off.

By God's grace, and out of total desperation, I immediately began to turn to Him in prayer. I was deeply impelled to reach for

Him, for the fear and pain were overwhelming. As I did, the long and painful – and quite necessary – process of transformation and illumination began.

I now see what was happening to me in those early weeks. I had become a convert of the "life must be easy and fun" movement. Convinced I would skate through life unscathed, I was going about my days living the typical American life, enjoying success building homes, seeing therapy clients and helping Laura with her business. We had plenty of money, a beautiful home, good friends, money in our IRA account – all was well with our life. And, as far as I was concerned, that was as it should be and would always be. Anything less than this was simply not in the cards for us. We were untouchable.

Over the years that message left me weak and vulnerable and I didn't know it. I had little emotional strength and was dependent on the conditions of life for my emotional well-being. Of course, I didn't see that in me at all. I thought of myself as well-prepared for hardship. My relationship with Christ was strong and foundational to my life. I was a man who invested time and energy into it to keep it that way. I was no superman, no doubt about that, but I suspected I would be able to step up and weather a storm if one might blow up. I was on top of it.

I didn't grasp the insidious power of my "expectation of easy" to, over time, erode away a spiritual base and leave me standing on shifting sand. It had taken hold and left me exposed, fragile. This trial of disease that was now upon us was all that was needed to knock the weakened foundation out from under me.

In the months following, through tearful prayer, God began to rip out of me the cancerous expectation, the demand that life be easy. It is not so much that I felt Him strengthening me – I didn't feel that.

No, rather, I felt Him breaking me, performing painful surgery to remove the cancer. This was difficult to grasp. I was looking for an infusion of strength and peace from Him. But He had to break me down to a point where I was willing to finally let go of this demand in my heart. He had to rip it out of my body. It was painful and bloody and messy. But it was only when I reached the point where I accepted that life is hard and deadly and I will never be immune to that – it was only when I finally gave into that that I began to rise to my feet again. And at that point, I began to find divine strength and peace trickle in to my soul.

Life is hard. Life is painful. Disease and tragedy are ever present, all around me. You might think I am despondent at that thought, that I am despairing and hopeless now. No. In fact, remarkably, I feel more peace than I have in the past. Because my peace now is not dependent on the conditions of my life. Before Laura's diagnosis, I had peace because I was confident I was one of those charmed individuals that would walk through this world untouched by serious affliction. I was trusting in luck, really. But my luck didn't hold and the storm broke in on us and we were battered by the winds and waves of disease. My illusion of exemption was destroyed. And at that point God became more real to me and the hope in Christ that has buttressed the souls of the saints for thousands of years broke through in a brilliant light. He really did have me and Laura in His sovereign grip and nothing could ever separate us from Him.

I can't go back to that safe place, that place where I am protected from the dark storms of life. There is no such place. It is a lie. But I am safe, nonetheless. Now, my safe place is found in God. For however black the skies and howling the wind, my soul is safe in Him. Nothing on this earth – no disease, no tragedy, no disaster

– can steal my soul, that eternal "me", from the grip of God. And when it is all said and done and my life is over, at the very moment of my death, I step over into the presence of God. At that moment, all of life's hardships and sufferings will be over, complete, and I will take my rest. Then, and only then, will I be finally and forever safe from the storm.

Suffering and affliction do not last. Suffering and affliction will not win. He will, someday soon, escort me to that true land of peace and I will enjoy Him forever.

August 29, 2017

32

A Remarkable Destiny

From within this space of disease and suffering, it seems my life has been cut off from me, taken away. The life I was enjoying on earth is gone and it is unclear that I will ever see it again. I suspect I won't.

In the early months that realization was devastating. It suffocated me. It was only when I began to, in the months following, deepen down into the truth of the great destiny I have in Christ that I started to recover from the loss of my life. Up to then I embraced the pop notion (though I was unaware that I had) that this earth life is the most important thing in all the world; that it is the only one I have and I had better live it with verve and gusto; that I am to treasure every precious moment because life is short and when it is gone, it is gone for good. There are no second chances. I must cherish each breath I take, each beat of my heart. Live to the fullest and squeeze everything I can out of this life.

It was this orientation that made the loss of my life so excruciatingly painful. And how could it be otherwise? If this narrative is true and the life I have now is unmatched, irreplaceable, all there is, then it is an unredeemable tragedy when it is spoiled by disease. Far from encouraging me to step up and live life fully, this orientation only served to press my face further into the miry pit. I couldn't breathe. Hopelessness was feasting on this feckless idea and I felt absolutely helpless to cut off its food supply.

Then, by the grace of God, I picked up a book by Presbyterian minister Dr. Timothy Keller titled *Walking With God Through Pain And Suffering*. Here was the life line I so desperately needed. Keller's message to me was simple and powerful: this earth life is not the only life I will ever live. In fact, it isn't even the best life I will ever live. For me, through Christ, the best life is still ahead – the best is yet to come. No matter how great I have it down here, this earth life cannot begin to compare with the glorious eternal life that awaits me in the Kingdom of God someday. It is like comparing a shot glass of water to the Pacific Ocean. The peace and joy and exhilaration that will envelope me when, finally, I stand face to face with Christ in His kingdom are incomparable. Words are wholly inadequate to begin to describe it. When all is done and my life is spent, my destiny – and it is truly a most remarkable destiny – is the Kingdom of God in all its splendor and glory. That is my true home, not this temporal cosmos, stained and contaminated by sin and death. This is a prelude, a preview, a warm up act. This is a tiny starter home, a small bungalow really. My final home is to be a palace in the Kingdom, living fully on a redeemed and glorified earth, inhabiting a glorified body that is no longer vulnerable to death and decay. All fear is gone because, in the Kingdom, God is finally back on the throne, His full glory having returned once again to earth, filling the earth and charging the entire cosmos, like before the fall. And I will live in my mansion in the presence of the reigning Son of God, a citizen of His kingdom and full heir to all the Father has handed over to Him.

This Kingdom existence will never perish or even fade away for sin and death are no more, having been once-for-all destroyed by Christ. The attending and ever-present fear and anxiety that dogged my every step during my mortal days on earth are gone. There simply is nothing to fear. Whether disease or violence or disaster or tragedy – these well-known companions have left my space and God finally exercises full control over it. Only His will has power and influence now. Neither sinful man nor hostile spiritual powers have any say about things. All is under His full authority, guided by His full presence in all He created. What was the domain of darkness and the world of the prince of the power of the air has been reclaimed by the Creator God. He has taken it all back and restored it, having put an end to the age of sin and death.

The more real this became to me, the more I came back to life. Now, all is well for I know this is my destiny! Nothing less than this. On that day, whether by death or His return, my mortal life on this compromised earth within this contaminated creation is swallowed up into eternal life. Like a butterfly emerging from its cocoon, I throw open my wings and fly into the eternal Kingdom of God. On that glorious day I am finally home, raised to new life, breathing the clear, crisp air of His Kingdom, enjoying His reign forever. That is my destiny. It is a most remarkable one to be sure.

September 1, 2017

33

Falling Up

Of course, from within the worst of the storm, it is hard to see clearly. My eyes are blinded from the intense deluge that relentlessly pounds at me. But on the back side of "worst", I begin to understand more broadly exactly what this experience of hardship is about for me and slowly find the words to capture it.

Several words and phrases come to mind as fitting descriptors: "breaking", "emptying", "yielding", "slogging". And another one that surprises me. The surprise comes in that it is not until much later, when we are free of the dark storm and on a path of recovery, that I understand its meaning: "falling".

This word certainly captures what I felt at the start of this struggle. It was as if I could not physically stand at times. The crush and weight were so great, my knees buckled. Each night, as I retired to the guest room, I would begin my prayer on the floor, on my knees, palms turned upward toward heaven. My body and spirit were on the ground. So, "falling" is very accurate.

Now, I am coming to understand my experience of falling more deeply and, thankfully, more completely.

My falling, during those harsh days before we went in for the transplant, was clearly a falling down. I struggled to keep it together, to stand and walk into the world and stay engaged in life. It all had come on us so fast – in a moment, our life was turned upside down and we had this specter of transplant staring us in the face. The path ahead was terrifying and we were told, within a month, that we would have to walk it and walk it very soon. This forced us to have to hold our normal, daily life in one hand, and this black, foul intruder in the other. It felt as if I was falling down into...well, into something dark and threatening and shapeless. People die from these transplants. Each day was a struggle to find some footing.

These matters are impossible to see from within the raging storm. I had to get above the clouds to gain some perspective. Now I see it.

For a solid year after her diagnosis I was falling down, flailing about, unsteady. But I was also, without understanding it, falling up (to borrow a phrase from author Richard Rohr). The up movement came every time I fell down on my knees and reached for God. I couldn't feel any "up" at the time, but it was there. Each time this affliction was pulling me down, God was pulling me up. Each drop down to my knees was also a drop up toward God. It was movement more deeply into Him and the great truths of what Christ has accomplished and will accomplish for those who trust Him. I was falling up into a more living faith in which God, the sovereign lover of my soul, becomes more real than ever before. I was falling up into a more true understanding of what this life on earth is all about. I was falling up into a vision of my life in this world stretching out in front of me, rising to life eternal and the Kingdom of God. And it is the falling up that has made all the difference in this. It has been my redemption.

This falling up was a work of God. I was not conscious of it and I wasn't choosing it. I didn't even know there was such a thing. It was a gracious work of God, initiated and advanced by Him on my behalf. He was reaching down, taking my hand, and gently pulling me up toward Him. What felt like the end of me was in reality the beginning of a new me with a new set of eyes through which to see the world and our life.

I think falling down and falling up are inextricably linked together. The one follows on the heels of the other, if I will let it. Of course I can miss the falling up aspect of the affliction if I never turn to God from within the pain and reach for His grace and power to carry me through. I can choose to put my head down and slog through it on my own. But if I lift my head and look up to Him – if I keep seeking Him, keep knocking on His door – He responds with a mighty hand to reach down and lift me up into Him.

Falling is an appropriate description because both falling up and falling down are processes that are beyond my power. The disease was so much more powerful than Laura and I and it was pulling us down. I could not prevent that from happening. It is the nature of the affliction. In fact, I think all afflictions are that way. Whether disease or tragedy or financial ruin or death of a loved one – when it comes upon you, it throws you down with an irresistible force. You are helpless, crushed under the weight.

But God, in His infinite lovingkindness, steps in and takes hold of you and begins to raise you up. At first it may be imperceptible. Yet as you move into the hardship, you slowly begin to feel a slight elevation. For me, it was the light streaming from two great realities that God used to pull me up: the total sovereignty of a loving God and the great hope of glory that awaits me in Christ one day. As that eternal light dawned in my understanding and in the deep of my heart, I could sense I was rising up, being lifted above the mud and grime. God in His mercy was meeting me in my brokenness.

My part was simple: I fell on my face in emptiness, seeking Him. And that's all it took. God rushed in to rescue. No, he didn't miraculously heal Laura of her disease. And, yes, she did have to have a stem cell transplant, and a risky one at that. I still struggled through it all, crying in the phone to friends at times, often carrying discouragement and fear through the day. Nonetheless, God filled me with the reality of His sovereign love and the hope of Christ and the Kingdom that lay ahead for us. And it made all the difference. My falling down was turned to falling up. And thank God I am still falling.

September 30, 2017

34

My Prayer

O God, help my unbelief. You have called me to uphold Laura and fight for her in prayer. Give me grace to do that.

O God, I need Your grace to believe, to see You in all this. Nothing transpires in our life but that You allow it and command it. Give me grace to know that deeply. Give me grace to see You in all Your love and glory and power in the midst of this trial. You love us with an unfathomable love, a love that extends forever, infinite and borderless. And You are in absolute control over all things in our life. From You and through You and to You are all things. All things! You always act for our good and turn all things to our good. You redeem all things in our life. All is well

O God, let me see and know that the best is yet to come. Some day You will call us to You in heaven and ultimately bring us into Your eternal kingdom, enjoying You and worshipping You forever. Our hearts will rejoice and be lifted up in such rapturous joy, nothing on

Earth can compare. Earth's greatest joys, most ecstatic moments, most brilliant bliss, are a thimble of water against the ocean of joy that is to be mine and Laura's when You call us home to be with You. Our true home is with You in Your kingdom. That is our glorious destiny.

O God, Thy kingdom come!

November 4, 2017

Made in the USA
San Bernardino, CA
18 March 2019